Rounds and Canons For Peace and Justice

by

Kenneth P. Langer

Book 16 of the Klangermuzik Series

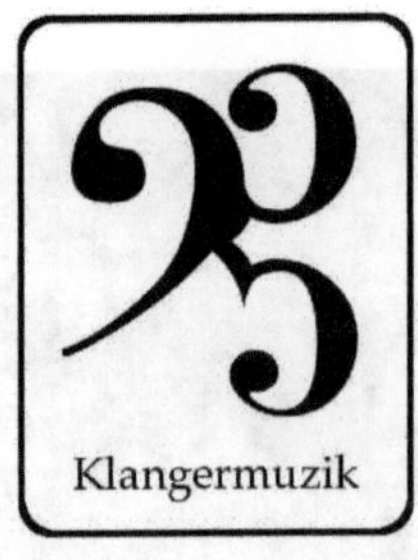

Rounds and Canons

For Peace and Justice

by Kenneth P. Langer

Klangermuzik.com

kennethplanger.com

First Edition (Softcover)

ISBN: 978-1-949464-10-8

Produced in the United States of America

The author may be contacted at klangerdude@gmail.com.

Introduction

Rounds and canons have been written and performed since at least the 12th century and have been a popular form of entertainment for singers. The reason is that they are easy to sing. Once a single line of music is learned, the entire piece can be performed.

Rounds and canons are known as imitative forms of music (the fancy musical term is "contrapuntal"). This is because they are created by having a line of music that is imitated by other vocal or instrumental parts at different times. When this is done, the notes of the original melody line up to create chords. A cleverly composed round or canon will be designed to be both interesting and pleasing melodically and harmonically. Rounds and canons can be for two or more voices.

Rounds

A round usually appears as a single line of music. In order for it to work as designed, however, the composer has to let you know how many musical parts there are and when they should begin. The composer must also indicate the timing for the entrance of each part. "Row Your Boat" and "Frere Jacques" are examples of rounds that are often sung by children.

In the example below, the numbers above the music indicate the place where each part should enter. In this case the composer has designed the round to be performed by at least four parts. The singers divide themselves into four sections. The first section would begin at number 1 (the beginning). When the first section reaches the number 2, the second section would begin at number 1. When the first section reaches the number 3, the third section would begin at number 1, and so on until all four sections have entered. For most rounds, the music is often repeated several times (which is where it got its name).

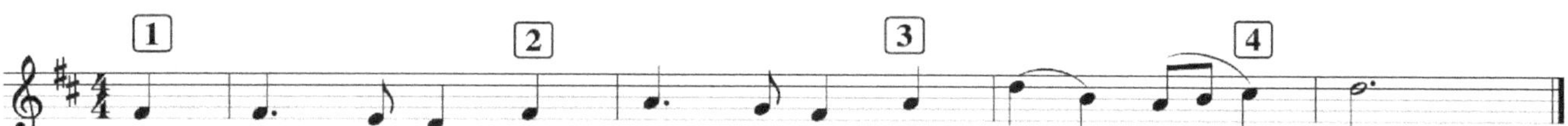

When done as instructed, the round will sound like the following example.

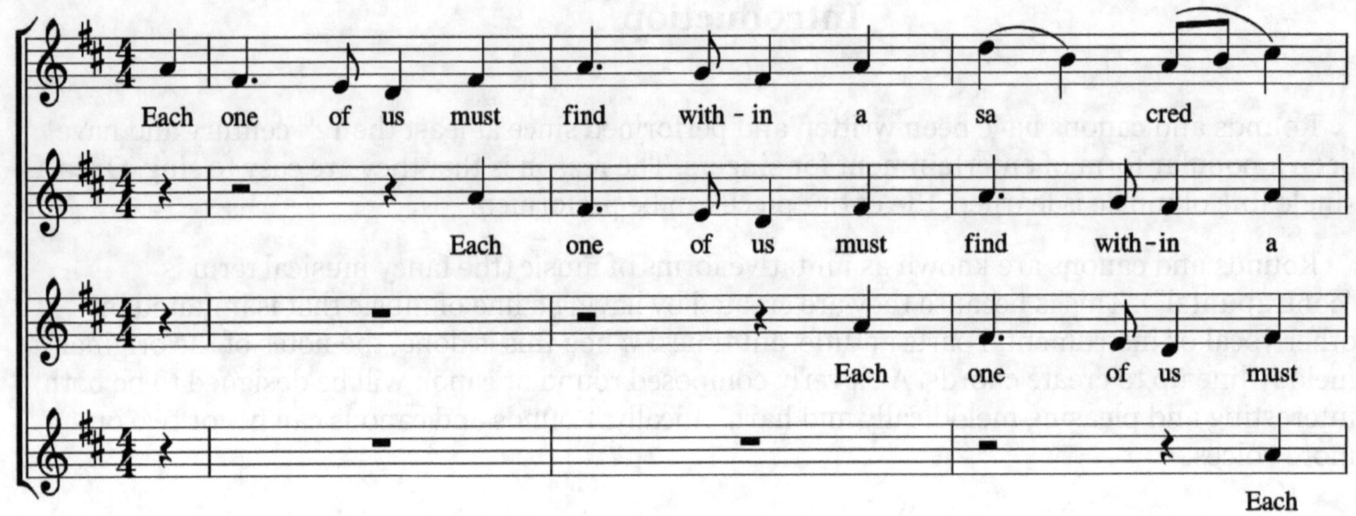

Canons

A canon is also a type of contrapuntal music. It is defined as a melody that is repeated at different intervals. Technically, a round is a type of canon. With the round, the melody that is repeated is always exactly the same. A canon, however, can be more flexible. Often a melody is repeated at a different pitch level (most commonly by a fifth). There are other ways to create variety in a canon as well. Perhaps the most obvious difference between rounds and canons is that canons are written out for all the parts and have a definitive ending.

The following is an example of the beginning of a canon.

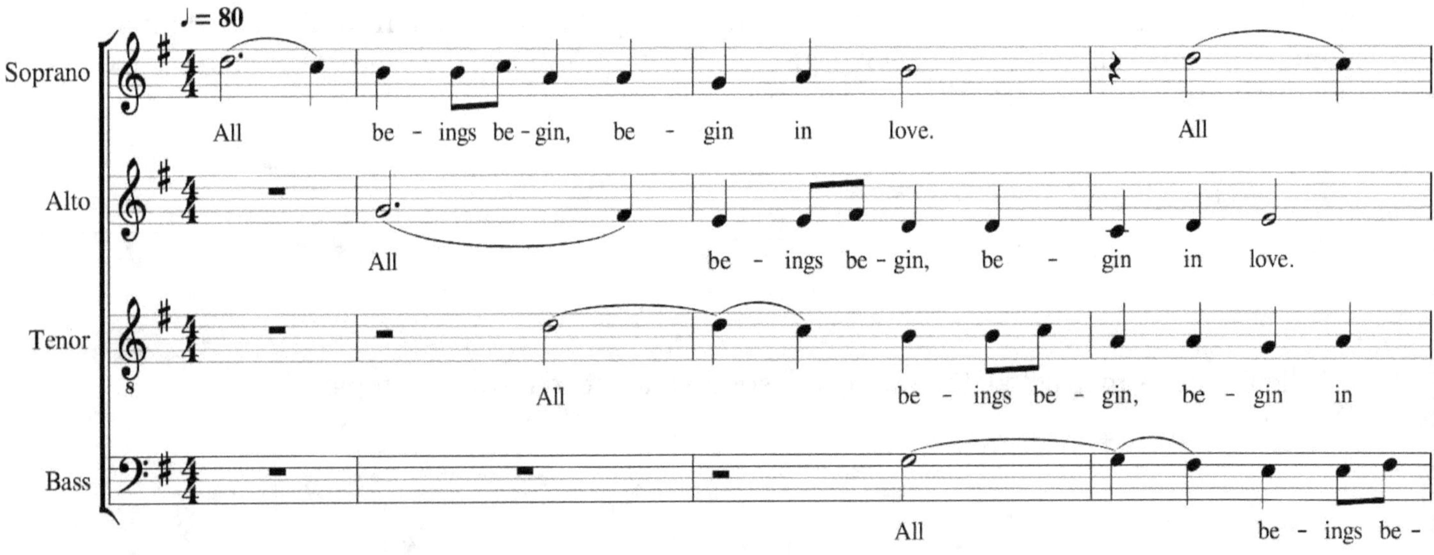

The Works In This Collection

All the works in this book are rounds and canons with texts that reflect concepts of peace and justice. Some have been adapted from other composers to fit new texts and some are original works. The works from other composers are all in the public domain. The texts come from adaptations of quotes from philosophers and theologians of many different traditions and backgrounds. The source for the music and text of each work is given.

All the pieces in this collection can be seen and heard through YouTube videos accessed from the website: http://klangermuzik.com.

Table of Contents

The Music

A Single Branch

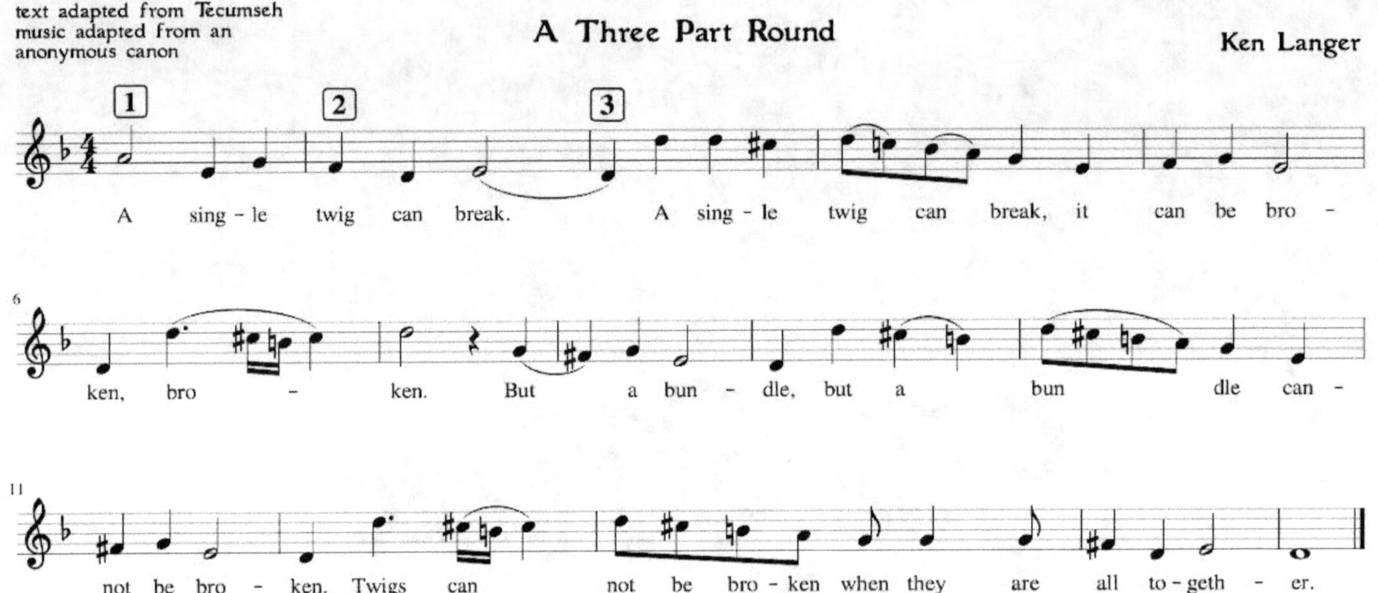

A single twig breaks, but the bundle of twigs is strong. ~ Tecumseh

A Thousand Ways

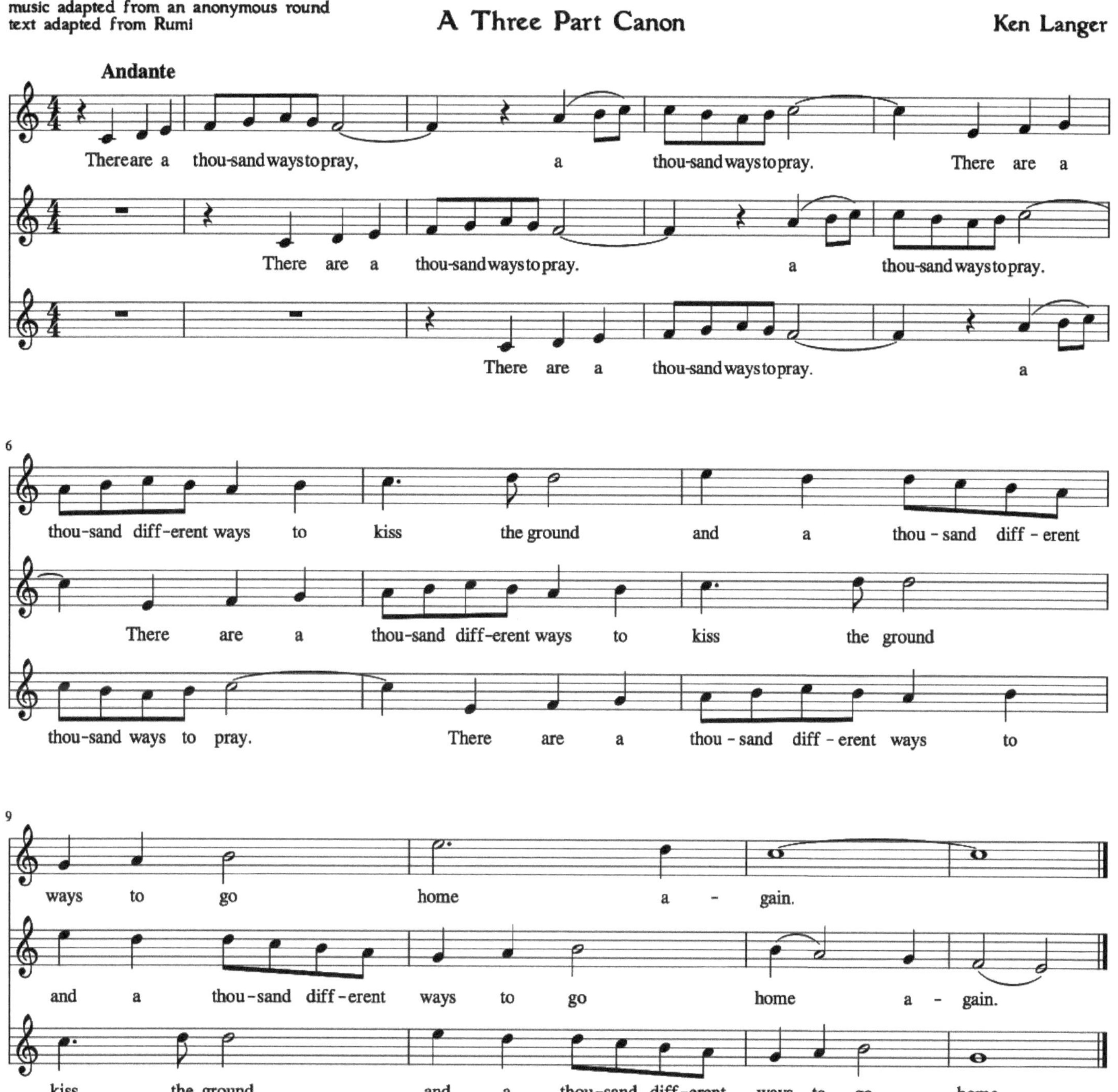

There are a thousand ways to kneel and kiss the ground; there are a thousand ways to go home again. ~ Rumi

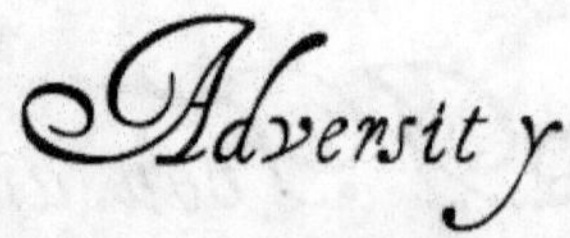

Text adapted from Malcolm X
Music adapted from an anonymous German Canon

A Three Part Canon

Ken Langer

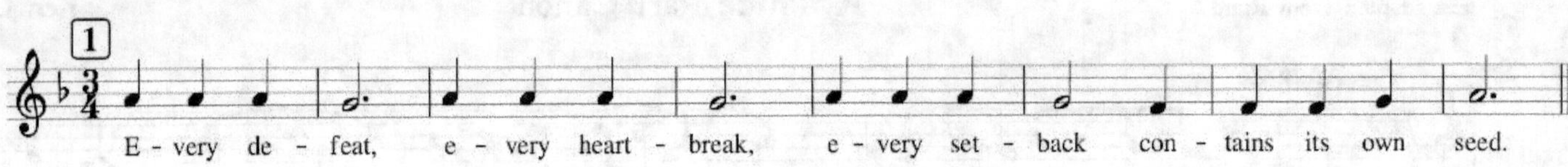

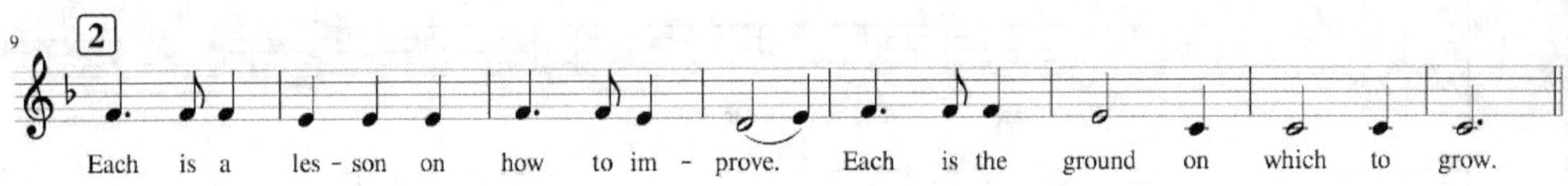

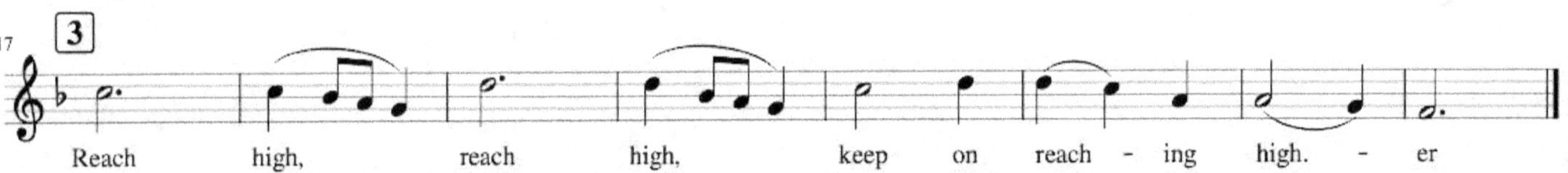

There is no better than adversity. Every defeat, every heartbreak, every loss, contains its own seed, its own lesson on how to improve your performance the next time.
~ Malcolm X

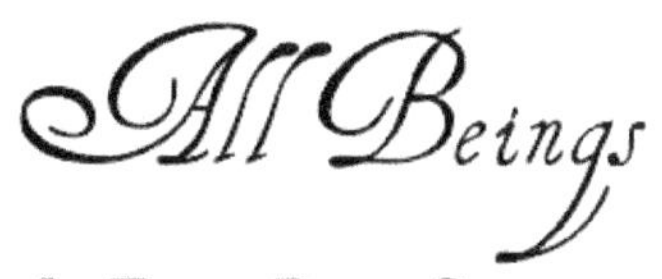

music adapted from John Blow
original text

A Four Part Canon

Ken Langer

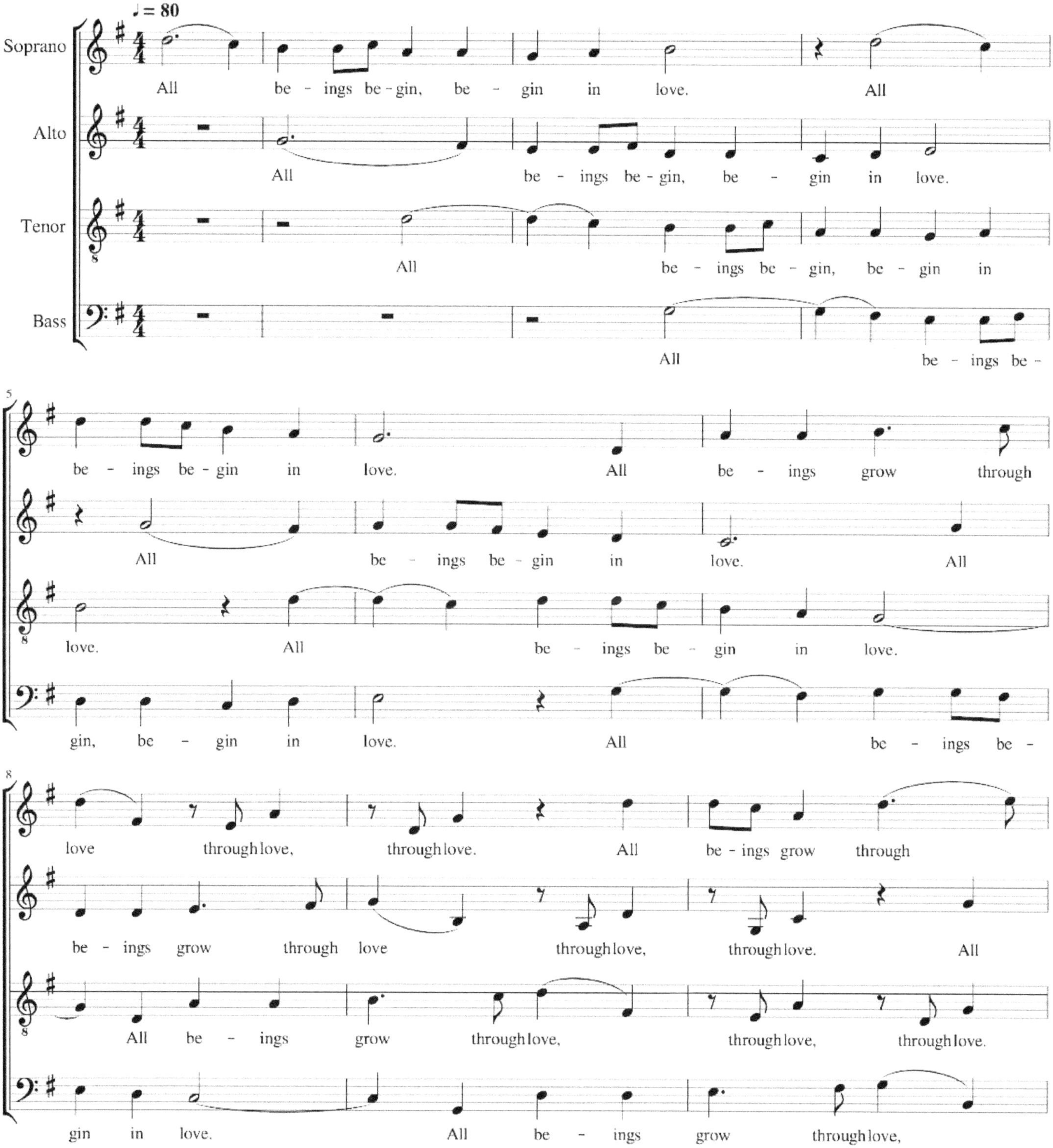

♩ = 80

Soprano: All be - ings be - gin, be - gin in love. All

Alto: All be - ings be - gin, be - gin in love.

Tenor: All be - ings be - gin, be - gin in

Bass: All be - ings be -

5

Soprano: be - ings be - gin in love. All be - ings grow through

Alto: All be - ings be - gin in love. All

Tenor: love. All be - ings be - gin in love.

Bass: gin, be - gin in love. All be - ings be -

8

Soprano: love through love, through love. All be - ings grow through

Alto: be - ings grow through love through love, through love. All

Tenor: All be - ings grow through love, through love, through love.

Bass: gin in love. All be - ings grow through love,

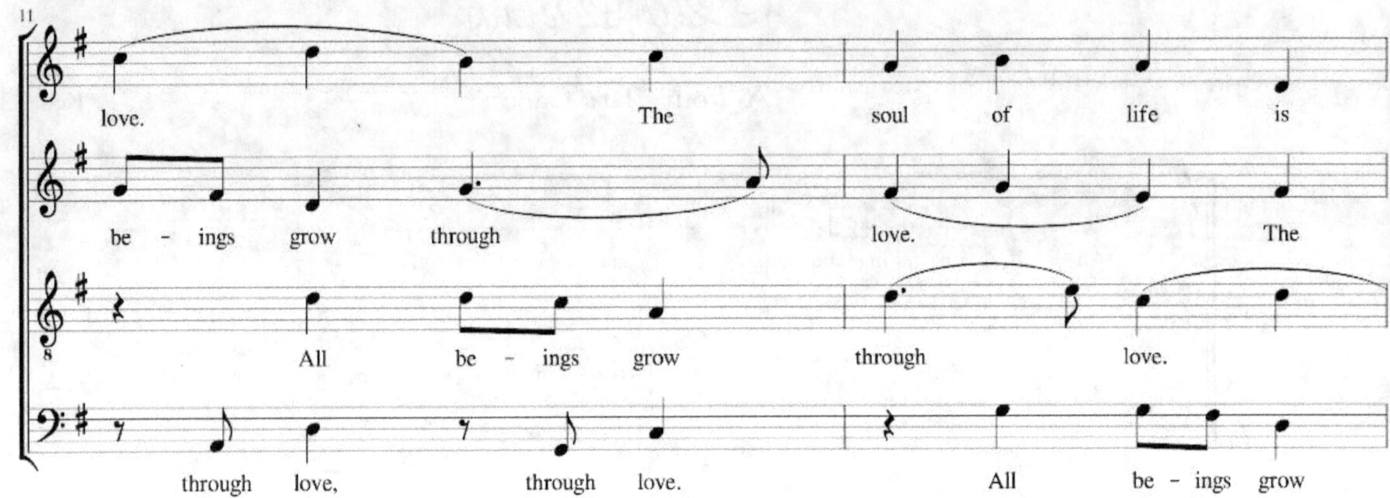
11
love. The soul of life is
be - ings grow through love. The
All be - ings grow through love.
through love, through love. All be - ings grow

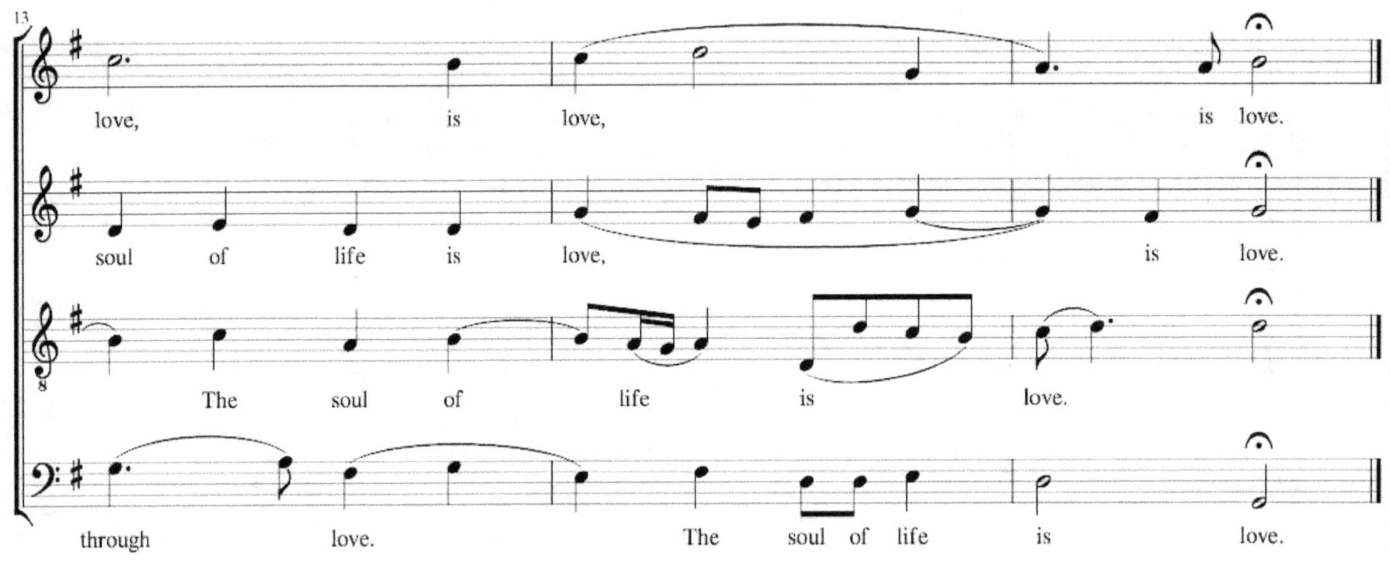
13
love, is love, is love.
soul of life is love, is love.
The soul of life is love.
through love. The soul of life is love.

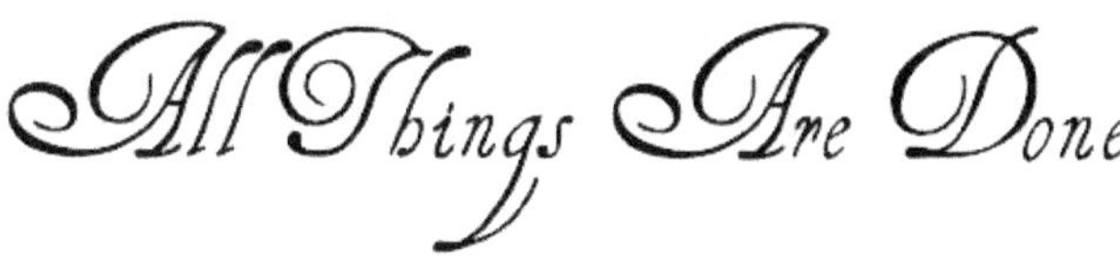

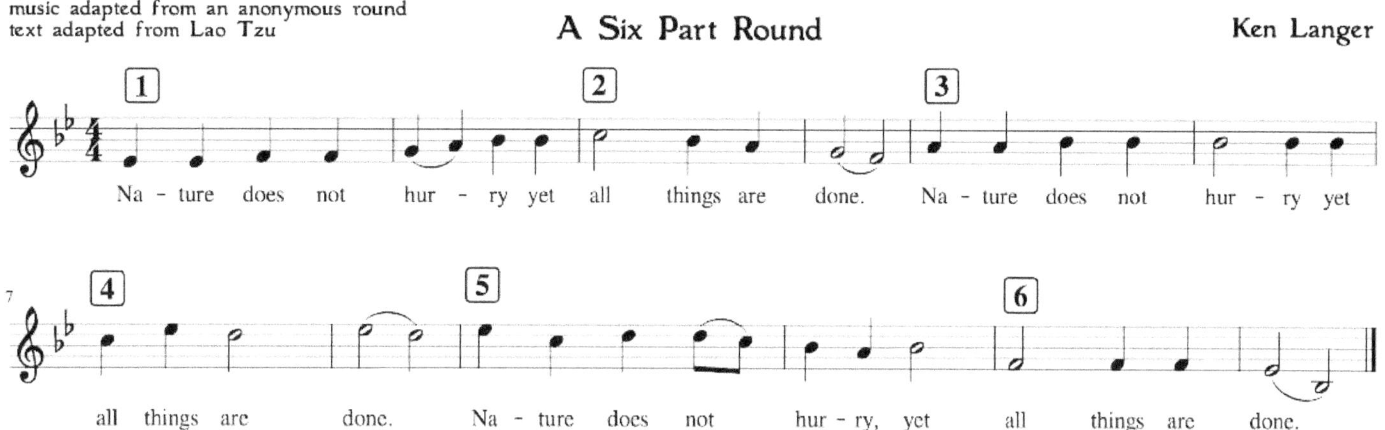

Nature does not hurry, yet everything is accomplished. ~ Lao Tzu

Always Prevail

music adapted from Rameau
original text

A Three Part Canon

Ken Langer

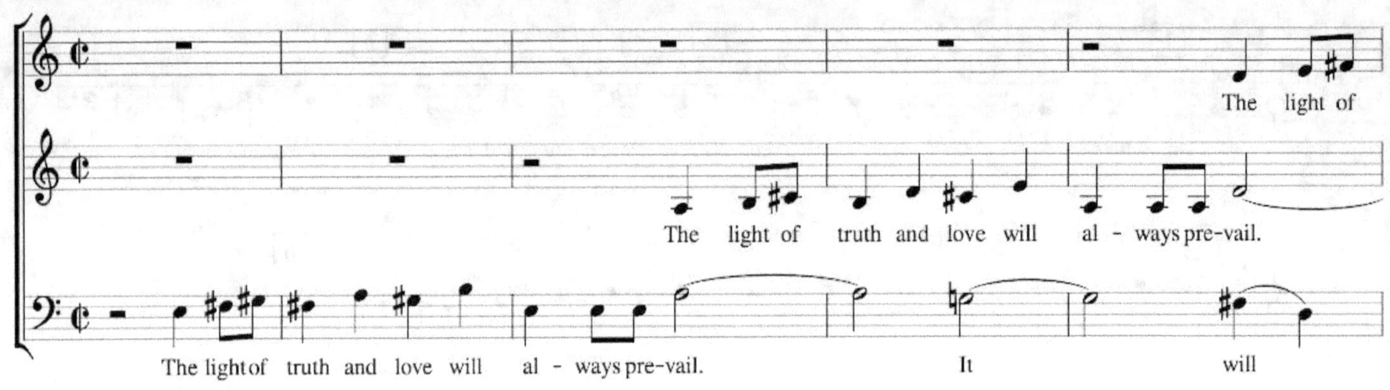

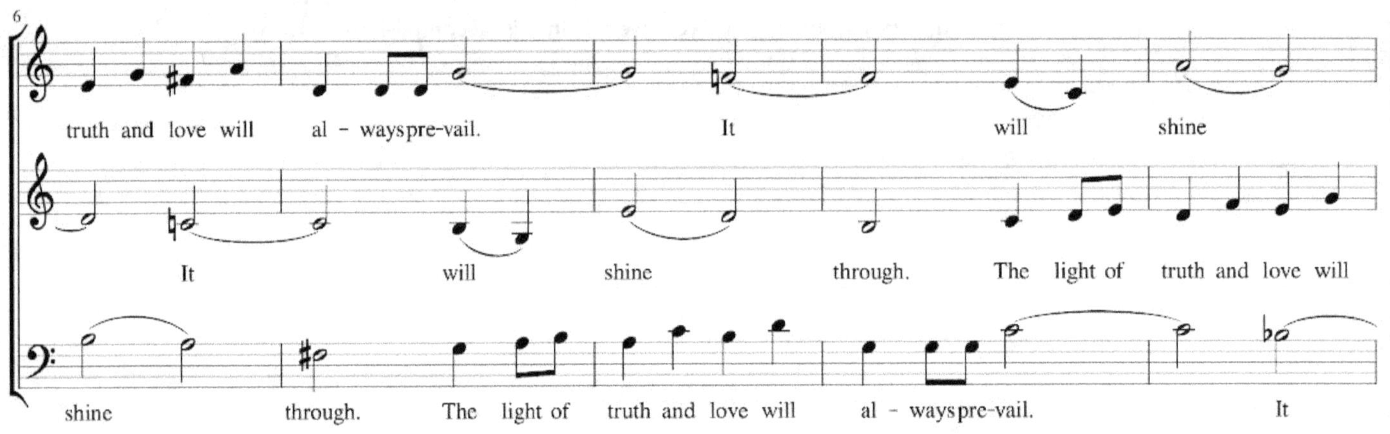

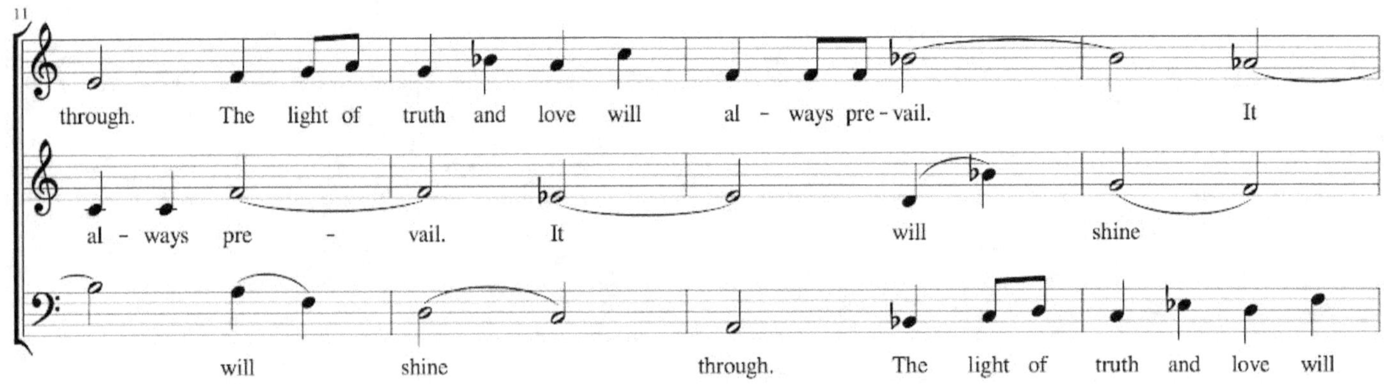

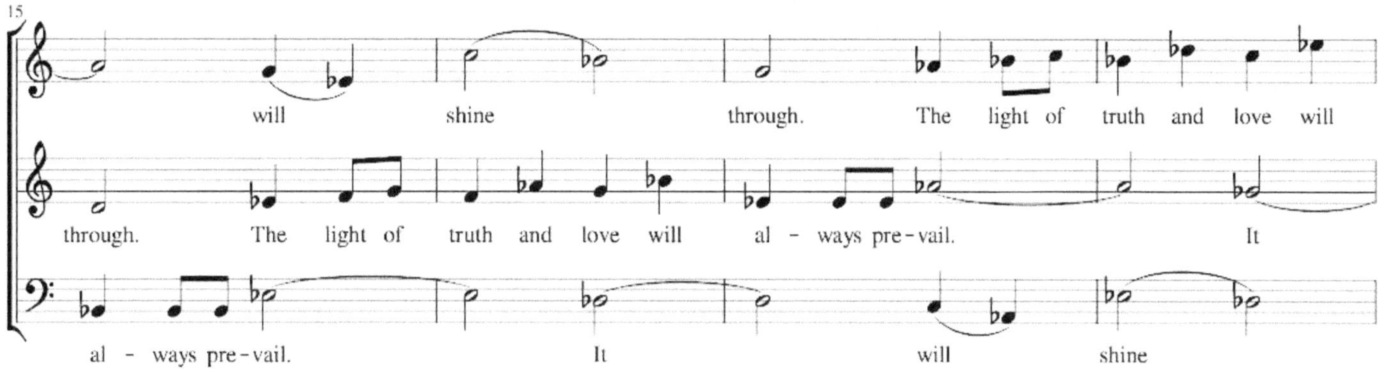
15
will shine through. The light of truth and love will
through. The light of truth and love will al - ways pre-vail. It
al - ways pre-vail. It will shine

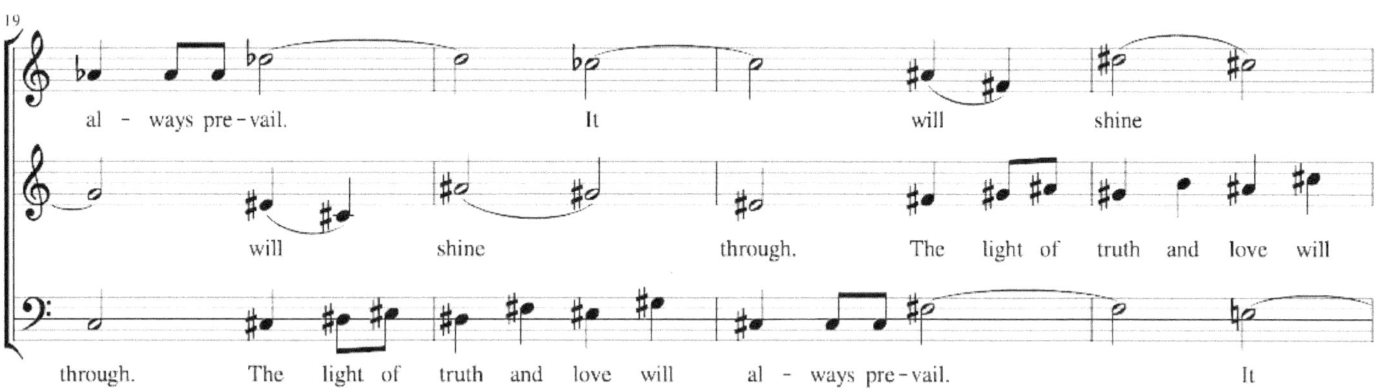
19
al - ways pre-vail. It will shine
will shine through. The light of truth and love will
through. The light of truth and love will al - ways pre-vail. It

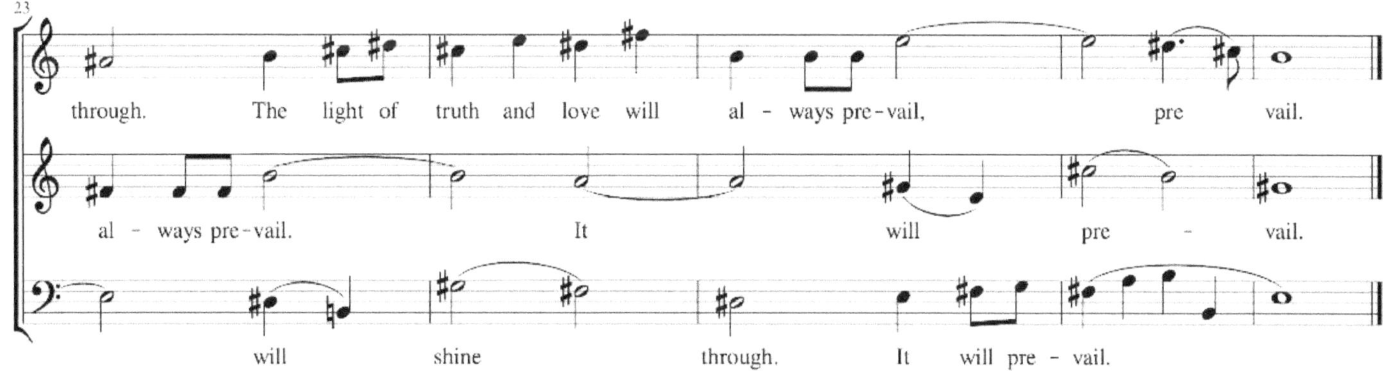
23
through. The light of truth and love will al - ways pre-vail, pre vail.
al - ways pre-vail. It will pre - vail.
will shine through. It will pre - vail.

An Awake Heart

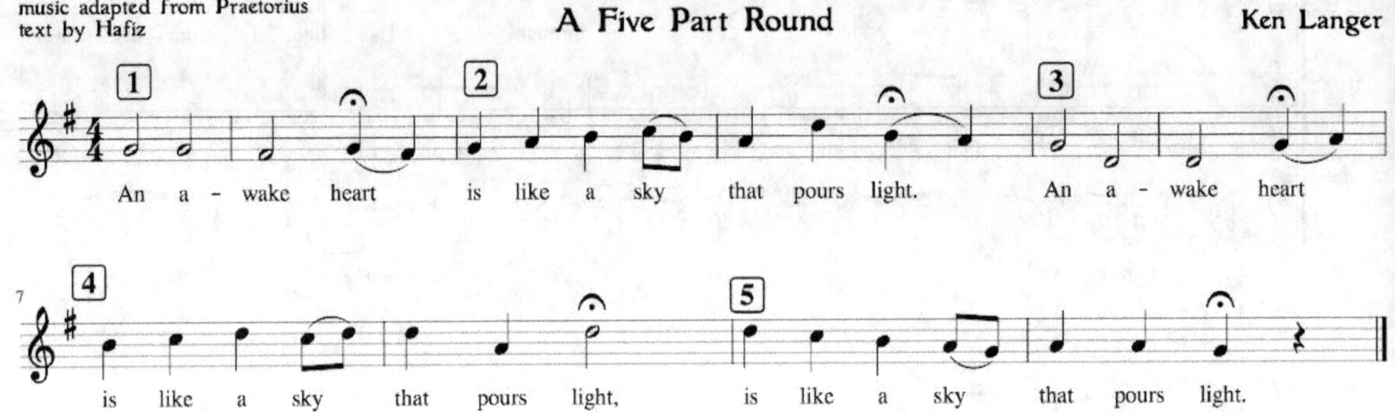

An awake heart is like a sky that pours light. ~ Hafiz

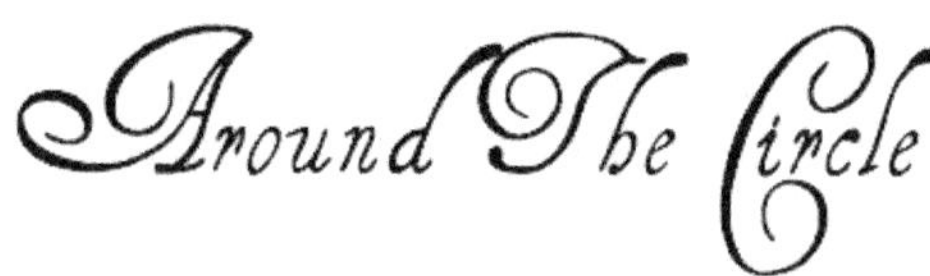

original music
original text

A Four Part Round

Ken Langer

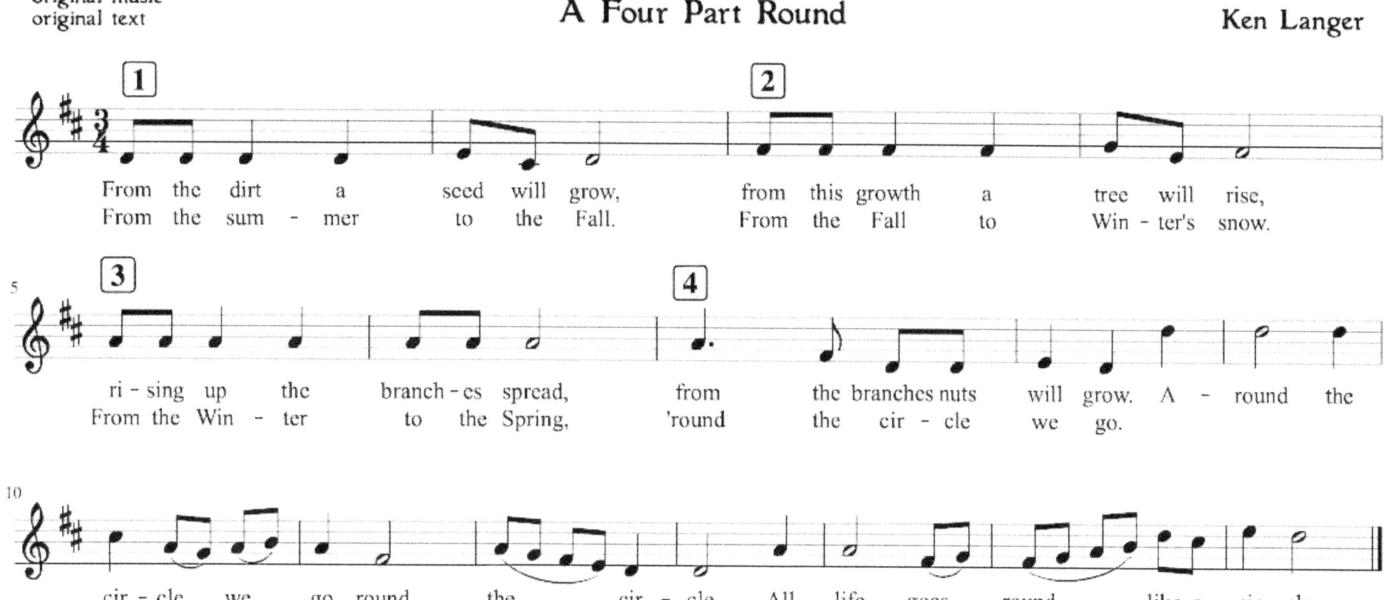

Better Than

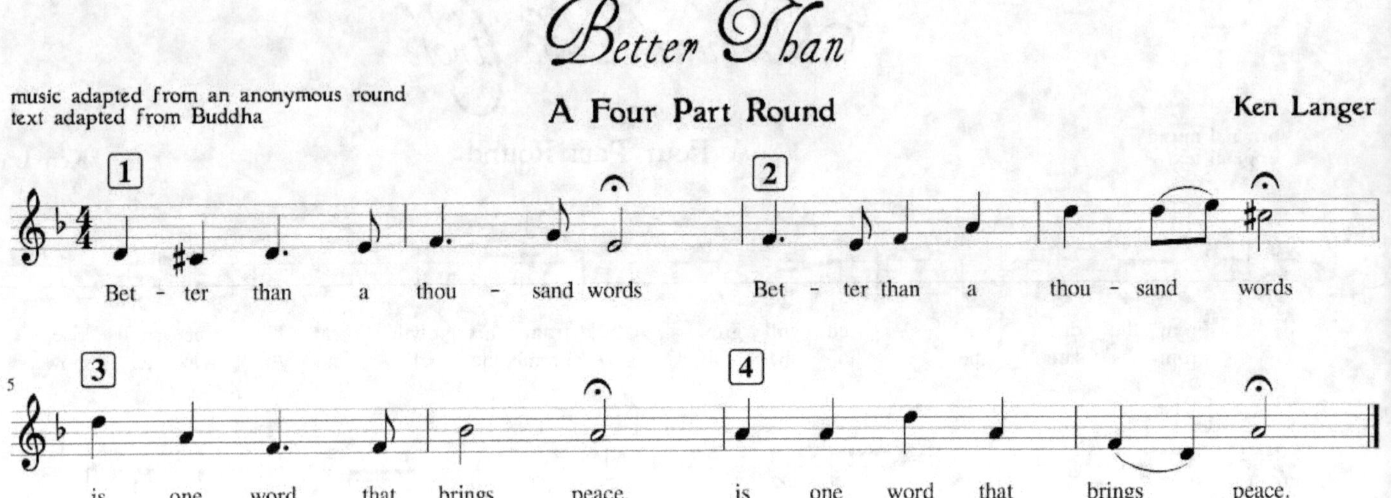

Better than a thousand hollow words, is one word that brings peace. ~ Buddha

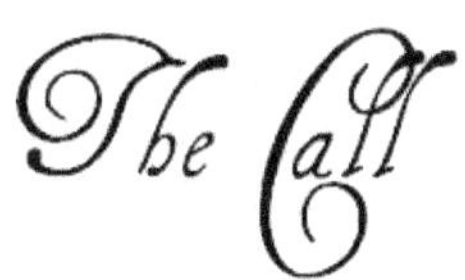

music adapted from Antonio Caldera
original text

A Four Part Canon

Ken Langer

Andante

1 The call of death is a call to beau - ty, a call to beau - ty. 2 The

7 call of death is a call to peace, a call to peace. 3 The

13 call of death is a call to truth, a call to truth. 4 The

19 call of death is a call to love.

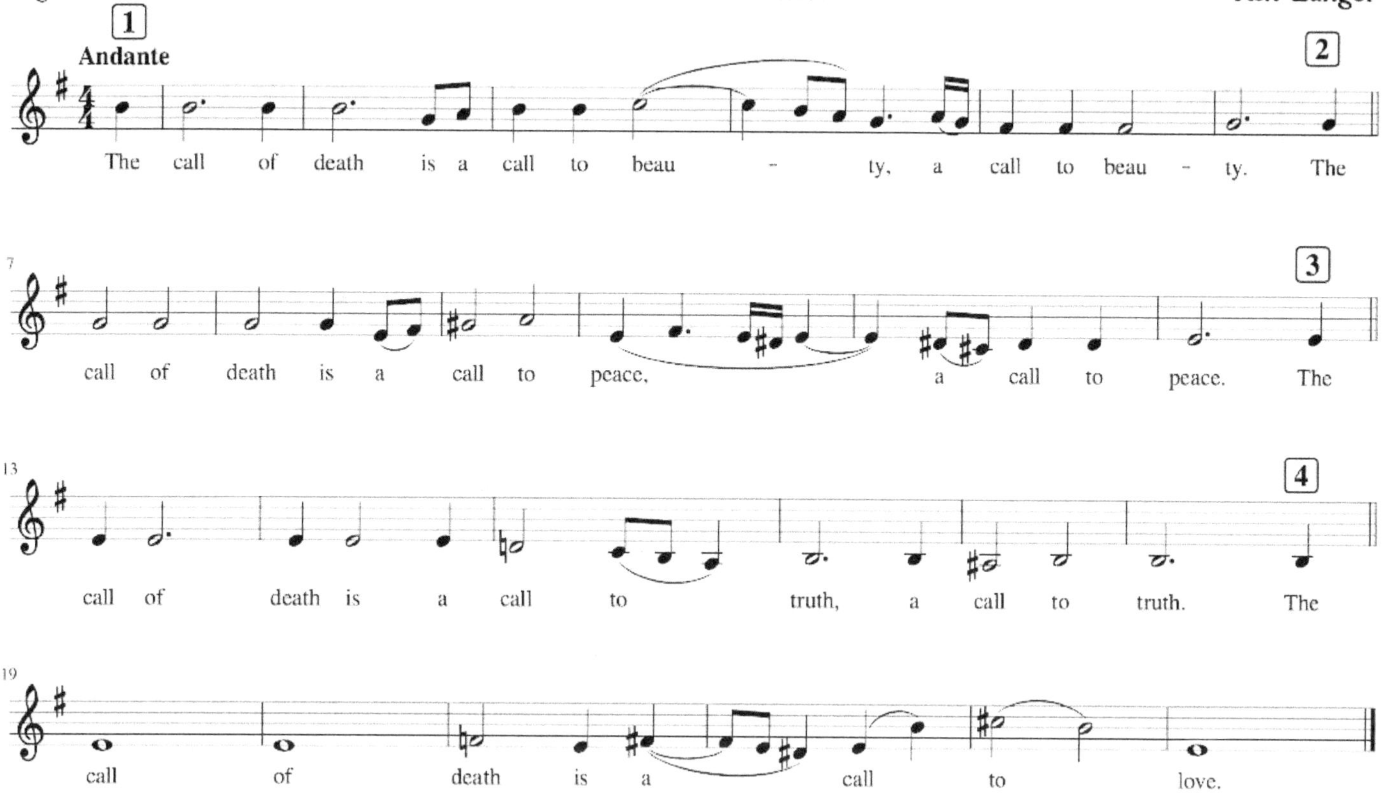

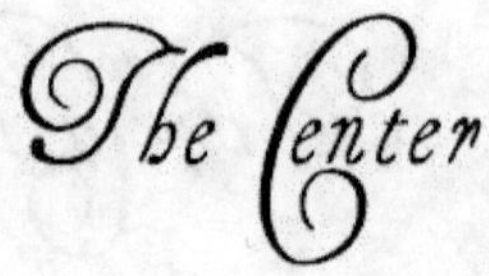

original music
text adapted from Martin Luther King

A Three Part Canon

Ken Langer

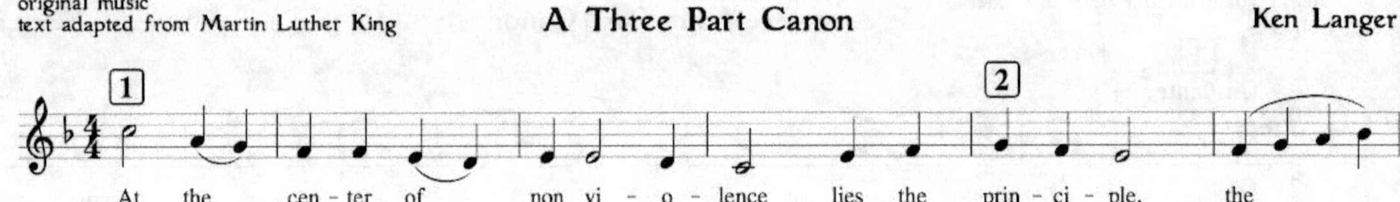

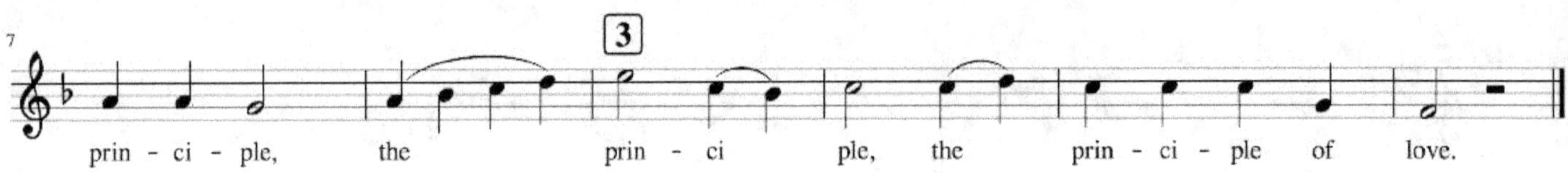

At the center of non-violence stands the principle of love. Martin Luther King, Jr

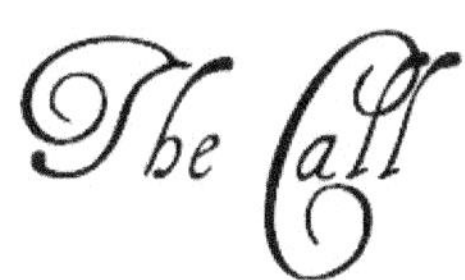

music adapted from Antonio Caldera
original text

A Four Part Canon

Ken Langer

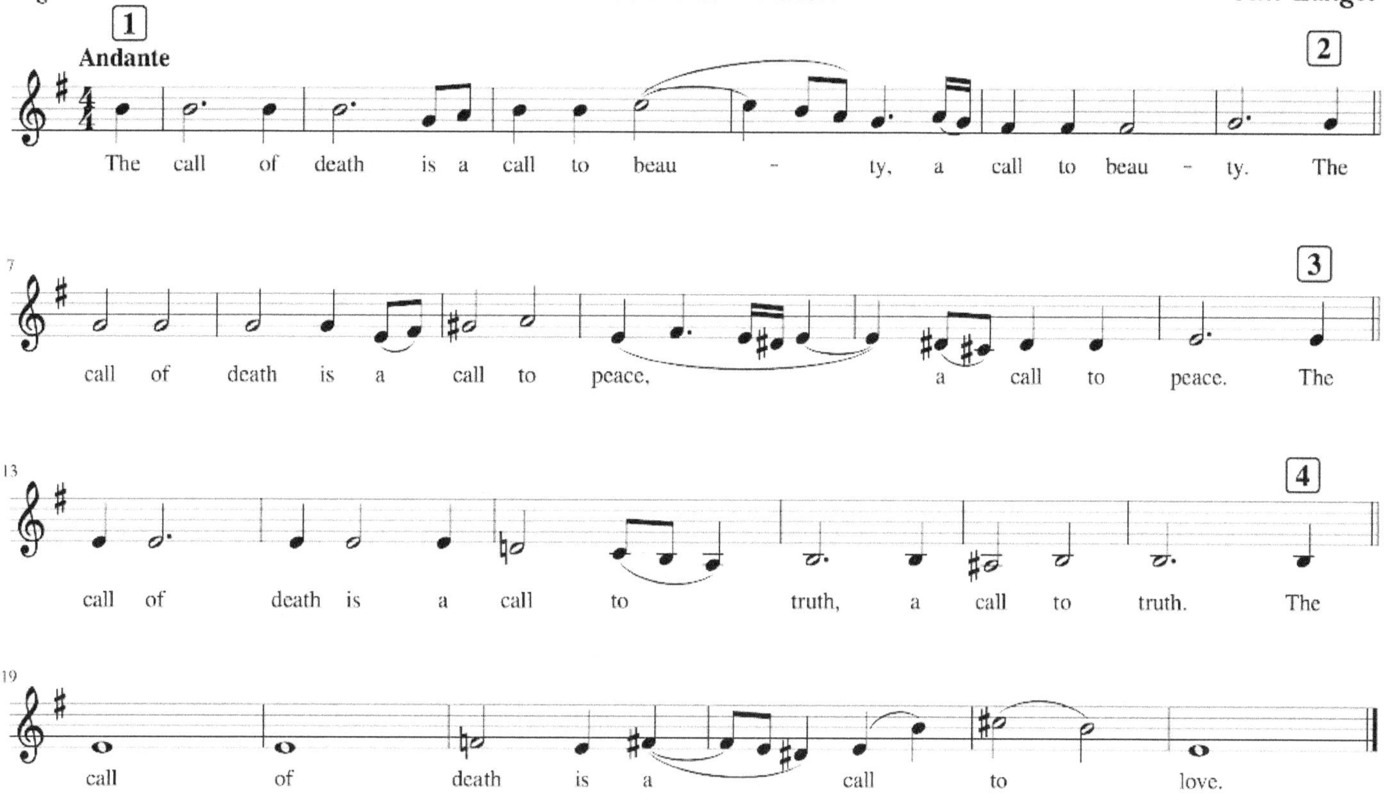

1

Andante

The call of death is a call to beau - ty, a call to beau - ty. The

2

call of death is a call to peace, a call to peace. The

3

call of death is a call to truth, a call to truth. The

4

call of death is a call to love.

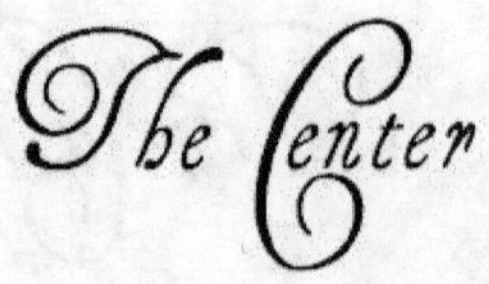

original music
text adapted from Martin Luther King

A Three Part Canon

Ken Langer

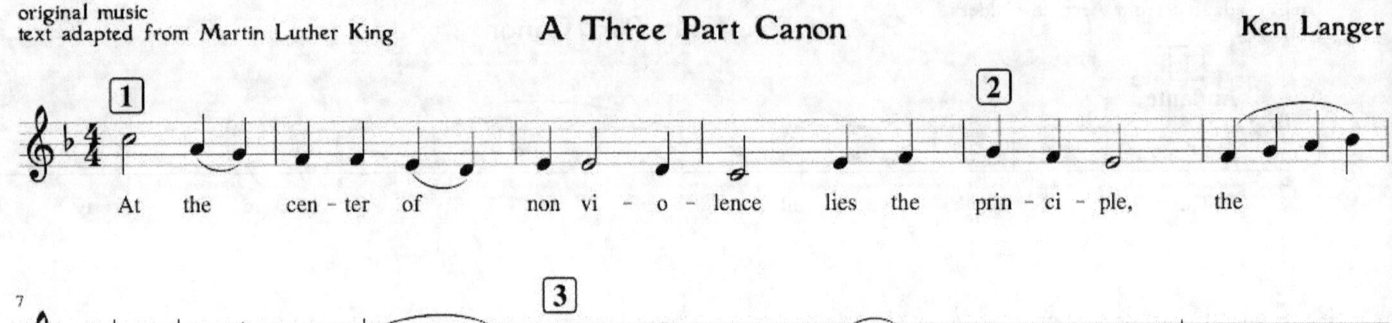

At the center of non-violence stands the principle of love. Martin Luther King, Jr

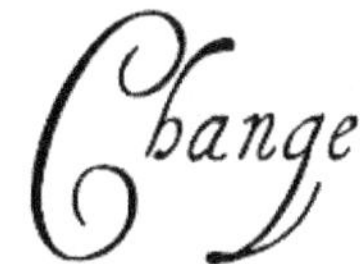

original music
original text

A Three Part Round

Ken Langer

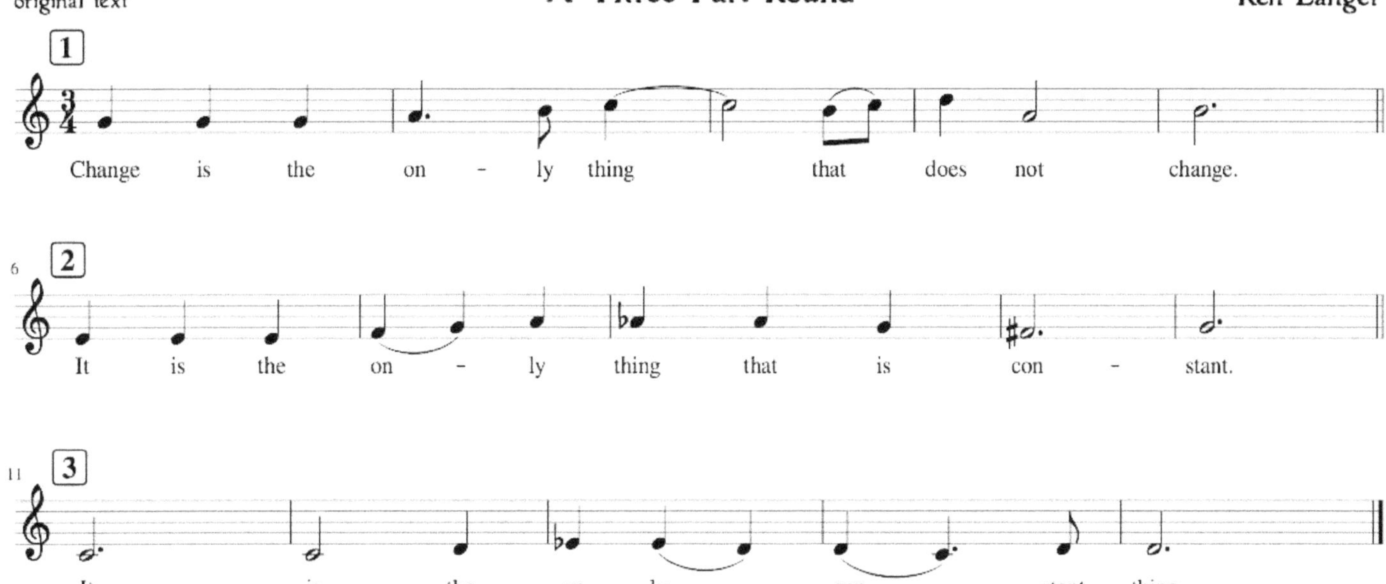

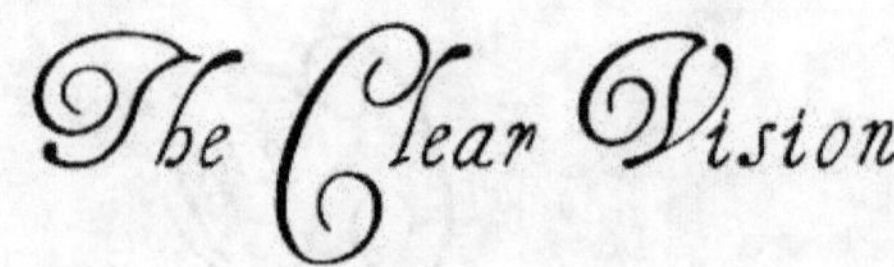

original music
text adapted from Carl Jung

A Three Part Jazzy Canon

Ken Langer

Swing ♩ = 110

The en - light-ened look with-in and the hope-ful look be-yond. and the
The en - light-ened look with - in and the hope-ful look
The en - light-ened look with - in

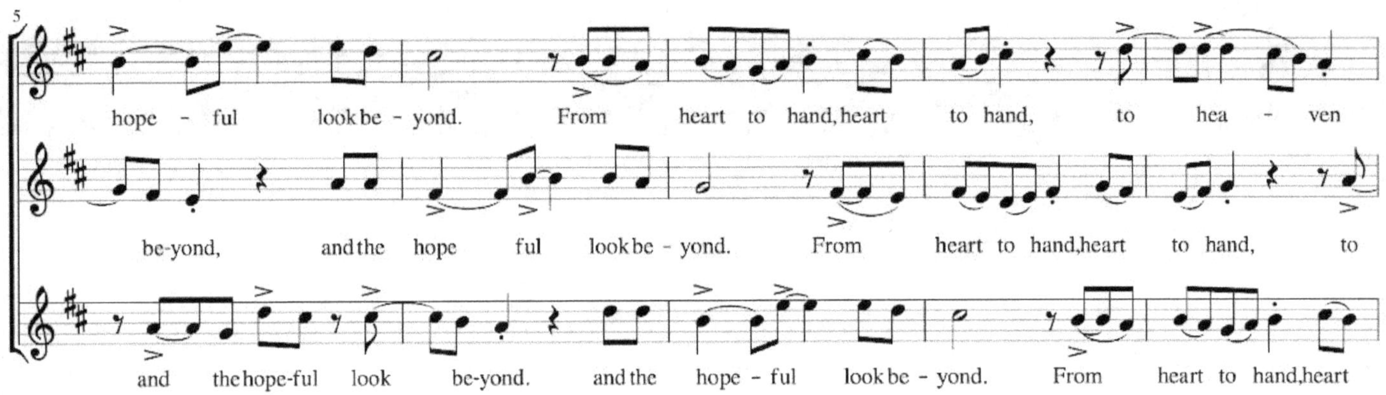

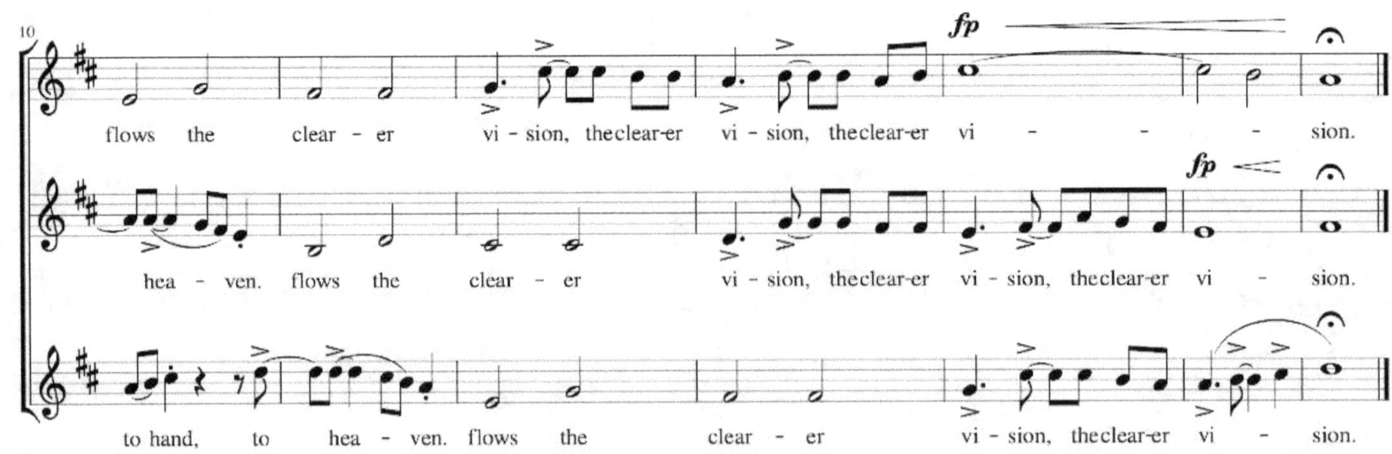

Your vision will become clear only when you can look into your own heart.
Who looks outside, dreams; who looks inside, awakes. ~ Carl Jung

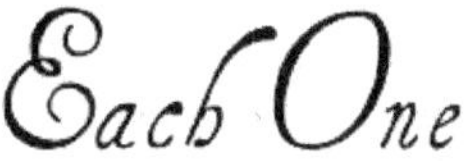

original music
original text

A Four Part Round

Ken Langer

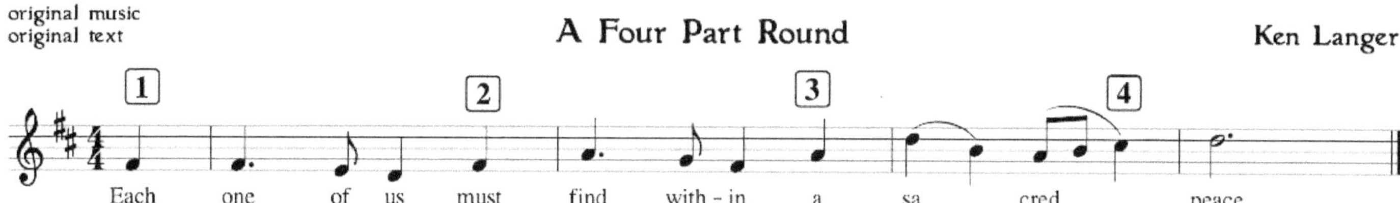

The Earth

original music
text adapted from Thich Nhat Hanh

A Four Part Round

Ken Langer

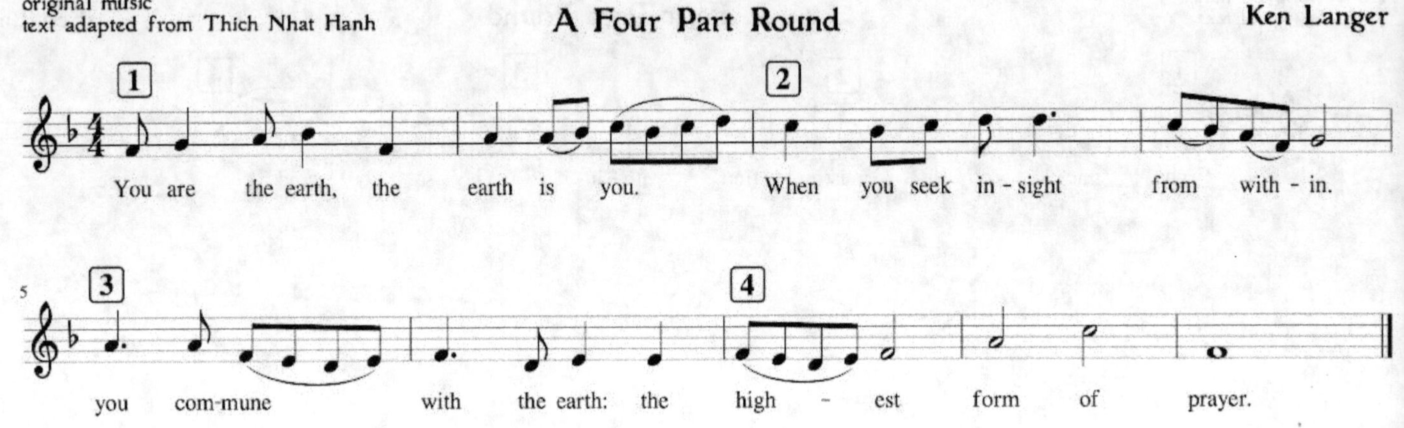

You carry Mother Earth within you. She is not outside of you.
Mother Earth is not just your environment.
In that insight of inter-being,
it is possible to have real communication with the Earth,
which is the highest form of prayer. ~ Thich Nhat Hanh

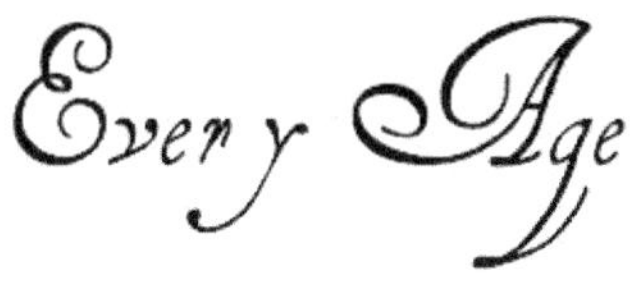

Text adapted from Ralph Waldo Emerson
Music adapted from an anonymous German canon

A Three Part Canon

Ken Langer

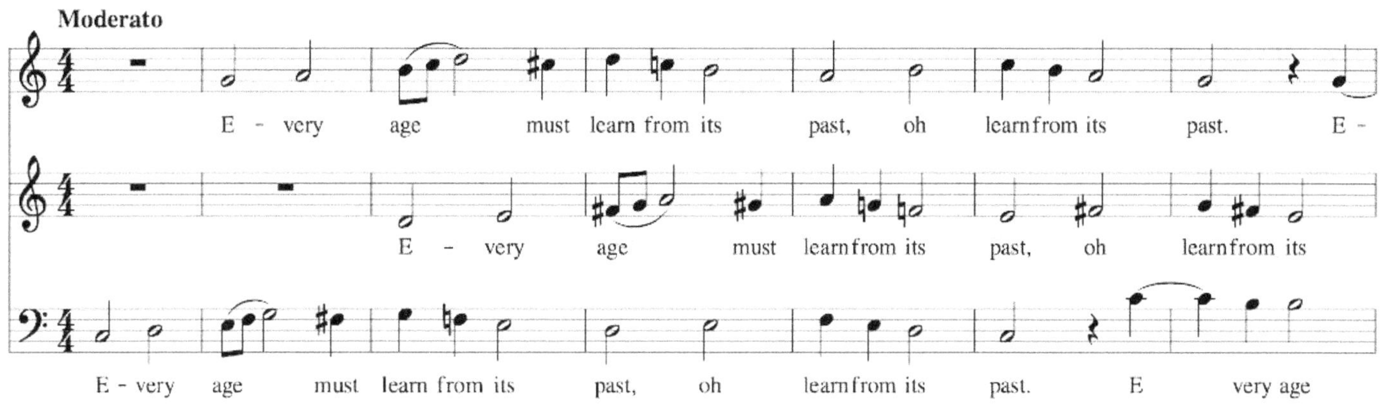

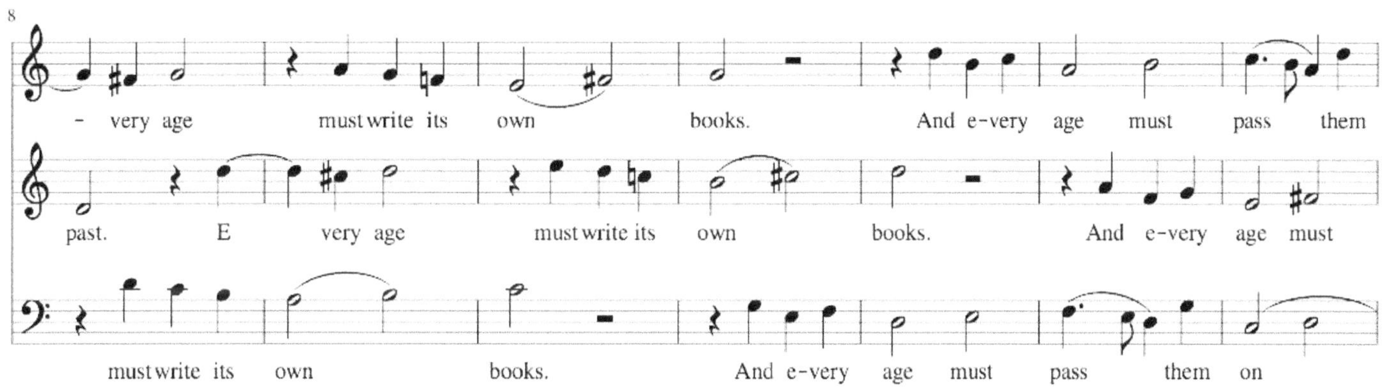

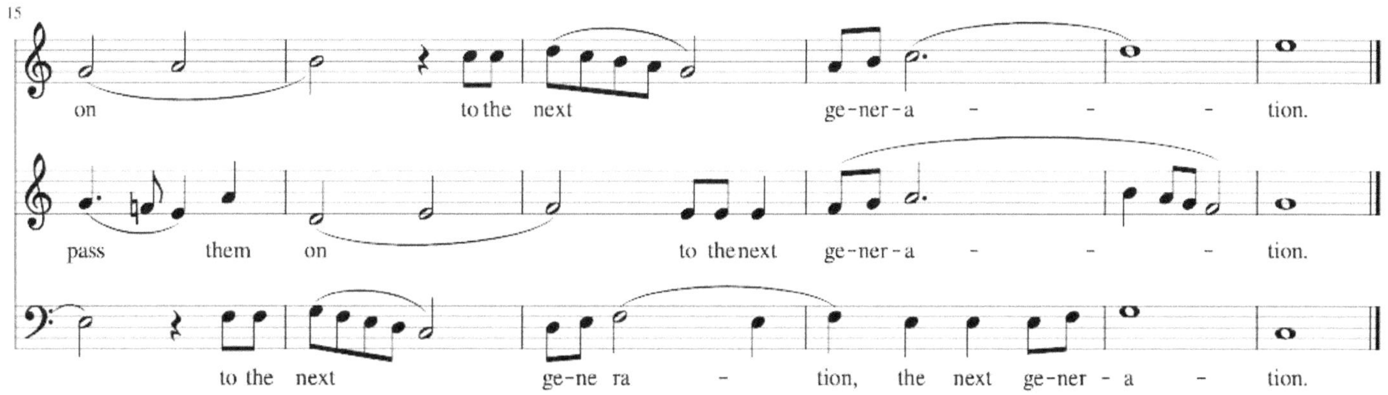

Each age, it is found, must write its own books; or rather, each generation for the next succeeding. ~ Ralph Waldo Emerson

Evil Triumphs

music adapted from Antonio Caldera
original text

A Six Part Round

Ken Langer

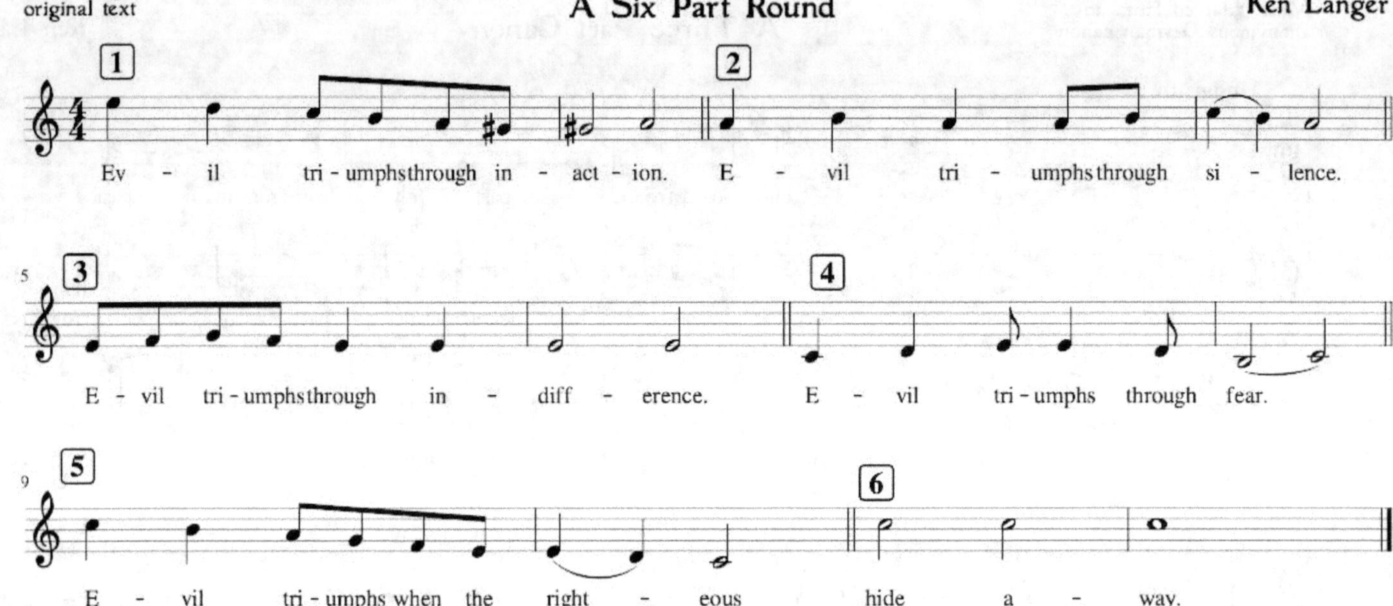

Find Peace

A Four Part Canon

original music
original text

Ken Langer

Moderate

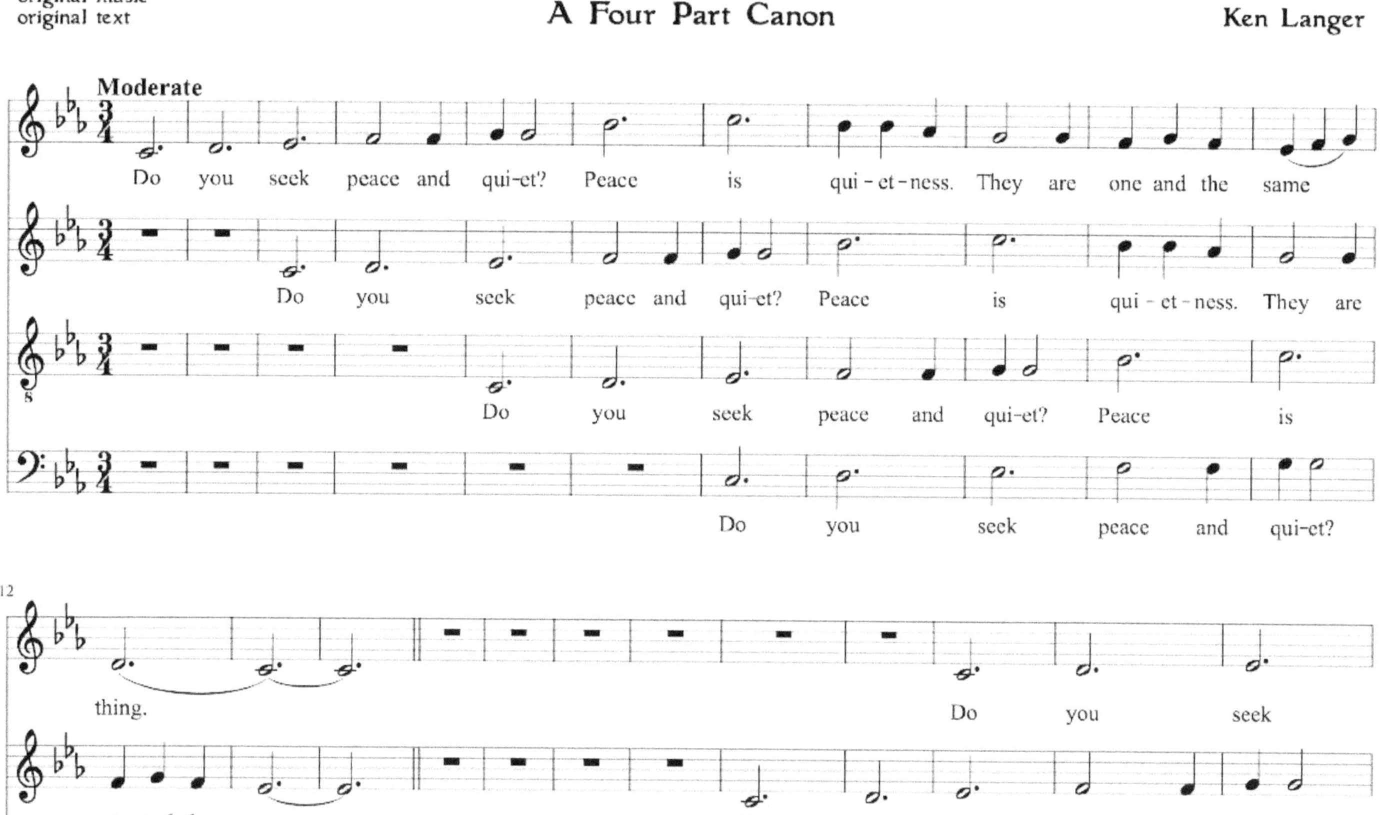

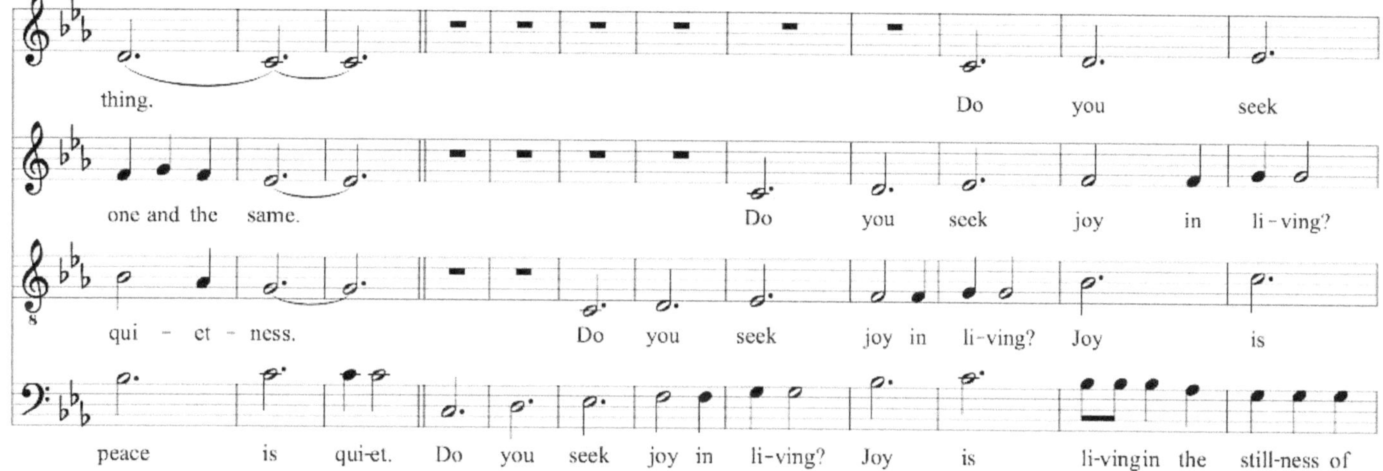

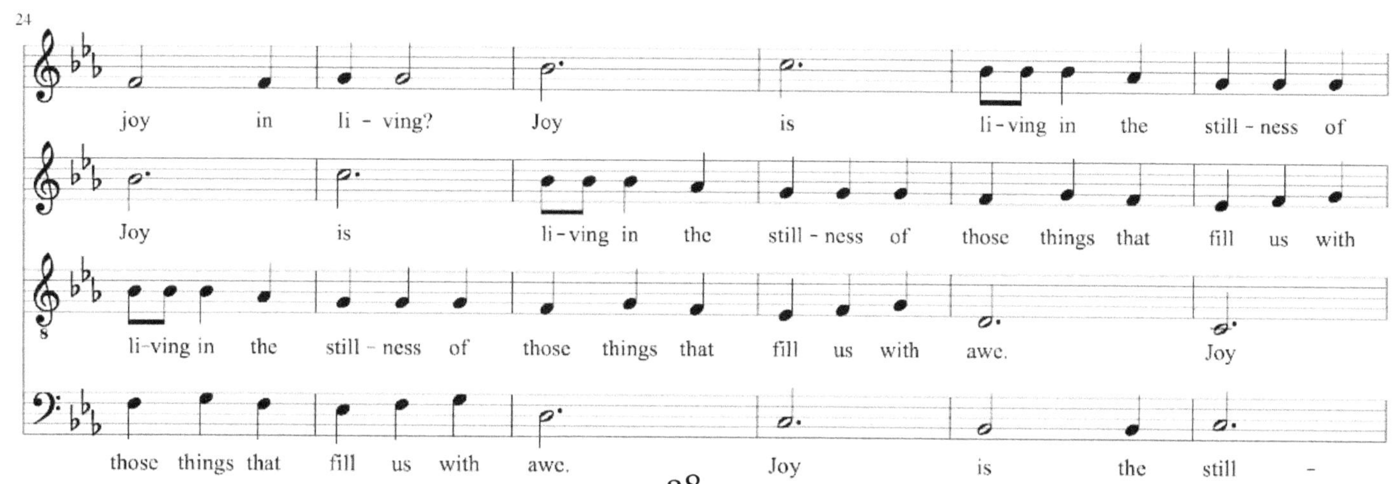

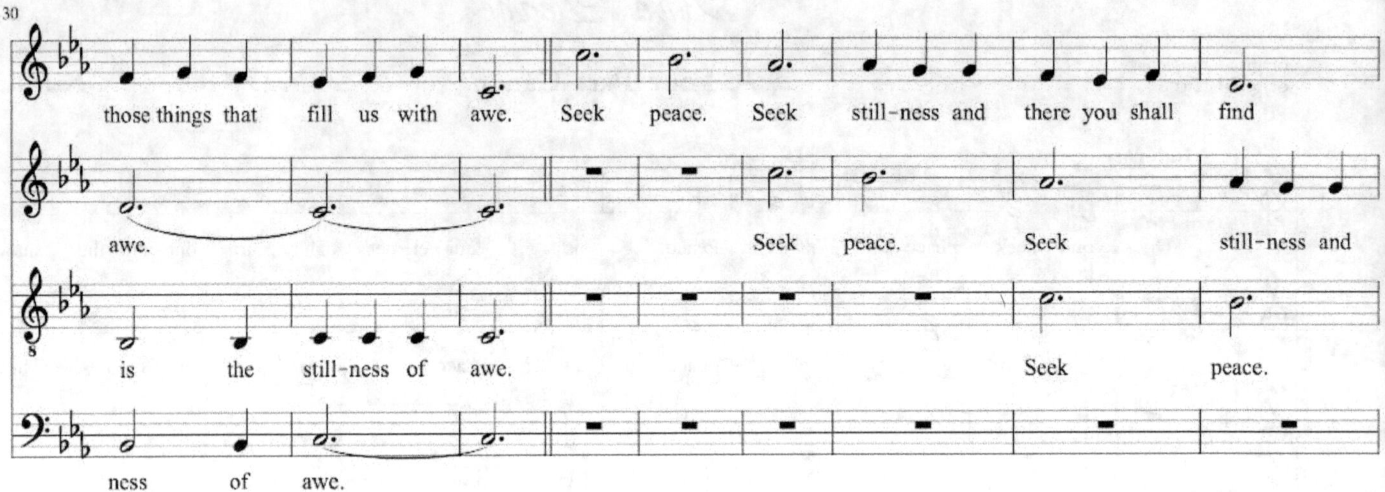
30
those things that fill us with awe. Seek peace. Seek still-ness and there you shall find
awe. Seek peace. Seek still-ness and
is the still-ness of awe. Seek peace.
ness of awe.

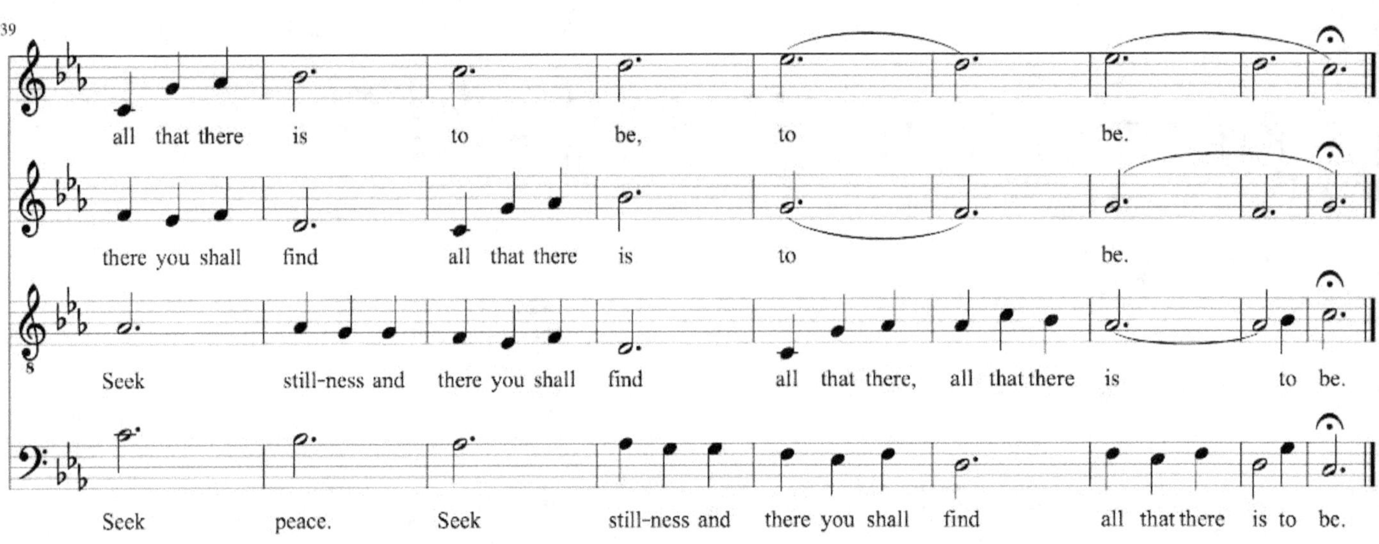
39
all that there is to be, to be.
there you shall find all that there is to be.
Seek still-ness and there you shall find all that there, all that there is to be.
Seek peace. Seek still-ness and there you shall find all that there is to be.

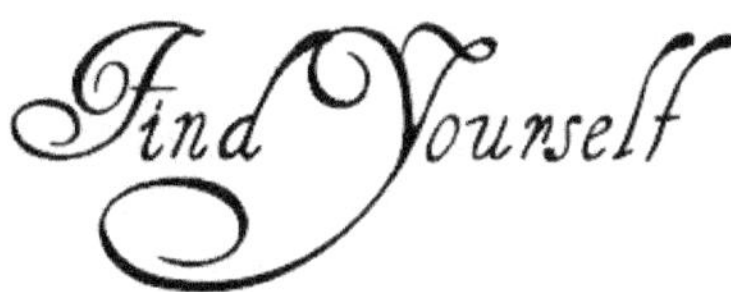

original music
original text

A Three Part Round

Ken Langer

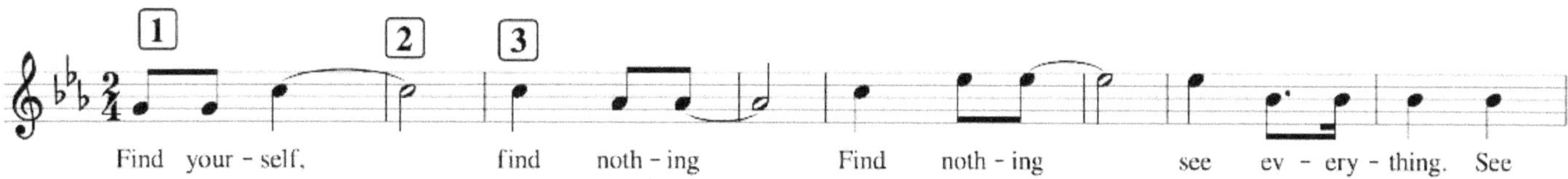

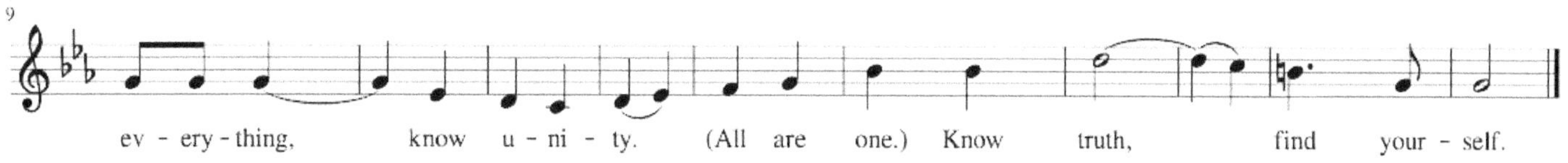

The Flowers

music adapted from Mozart
text adapted from May Sarton

A Three Part Canon

Ken Langer

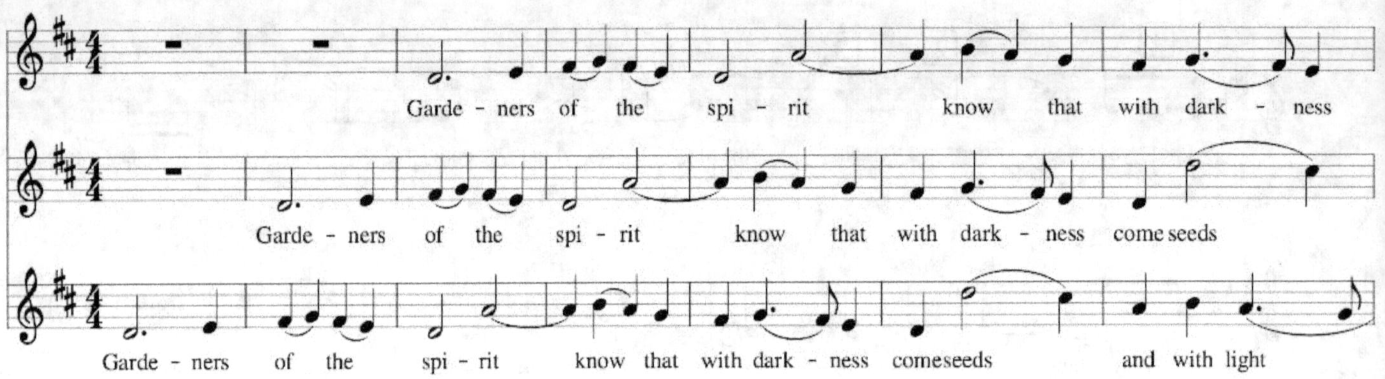

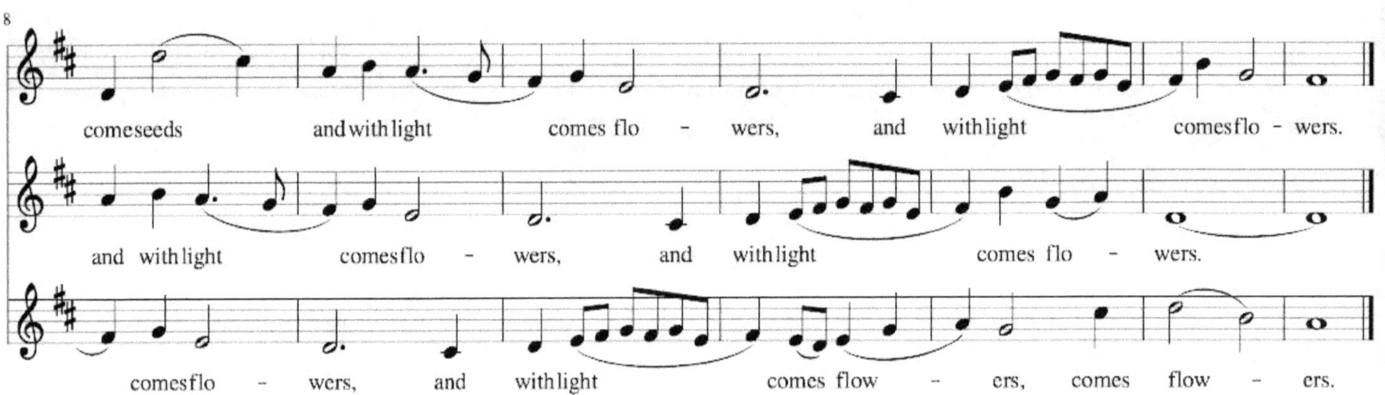

Help us to be ever faithful gardeners of the spirit, who know that without darkness nothing comes to birth, and without light nothing flowers. ~ May Sarton

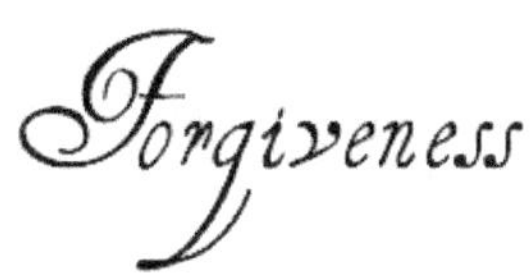

music adapted froman anonymous round
text adapted from Martin Luther King

A Four Part Round

Ken Langer

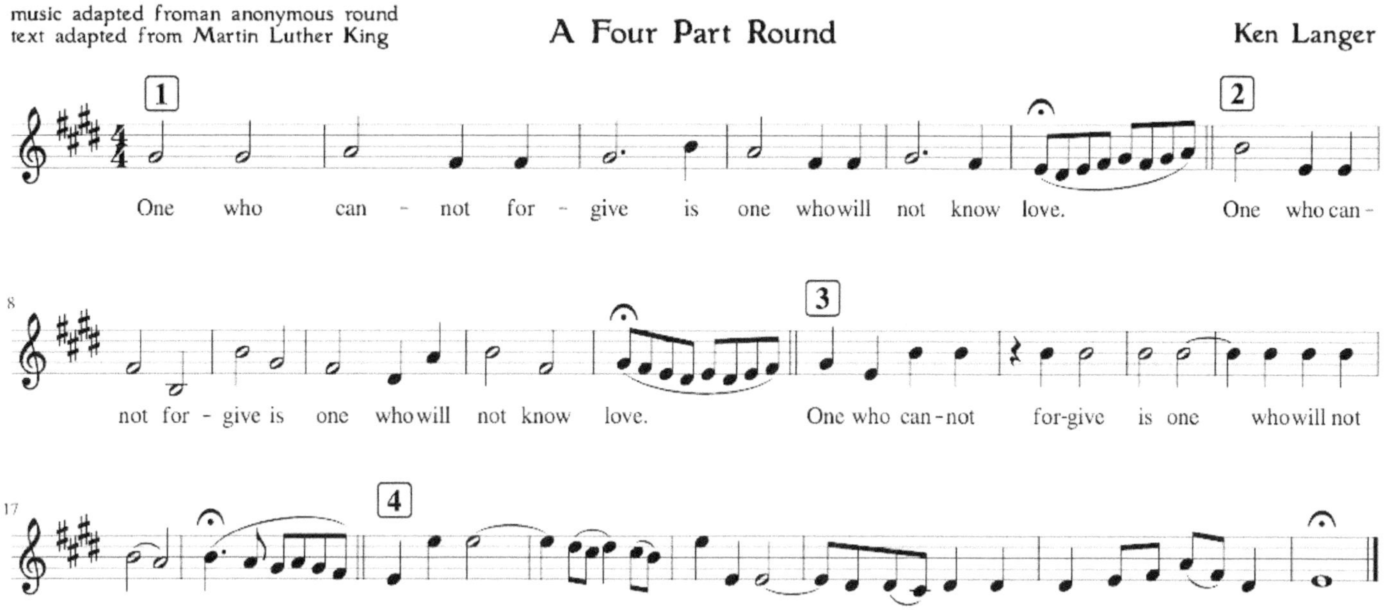

We must develop and maintain the capacity to forgive.
He who is devoid of the power to forgive is devoid of the power to love.
There is some good in the worst of us and some evil in the best of us.
When we discover this, we are less prone to hate our enemies. ~ Martin Luther King, Jr.

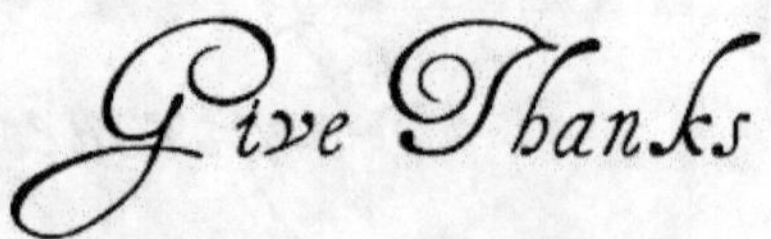

music adapted from William Boyce
text adapted from Tecumseh

A Four Part Canon

Ken Langer

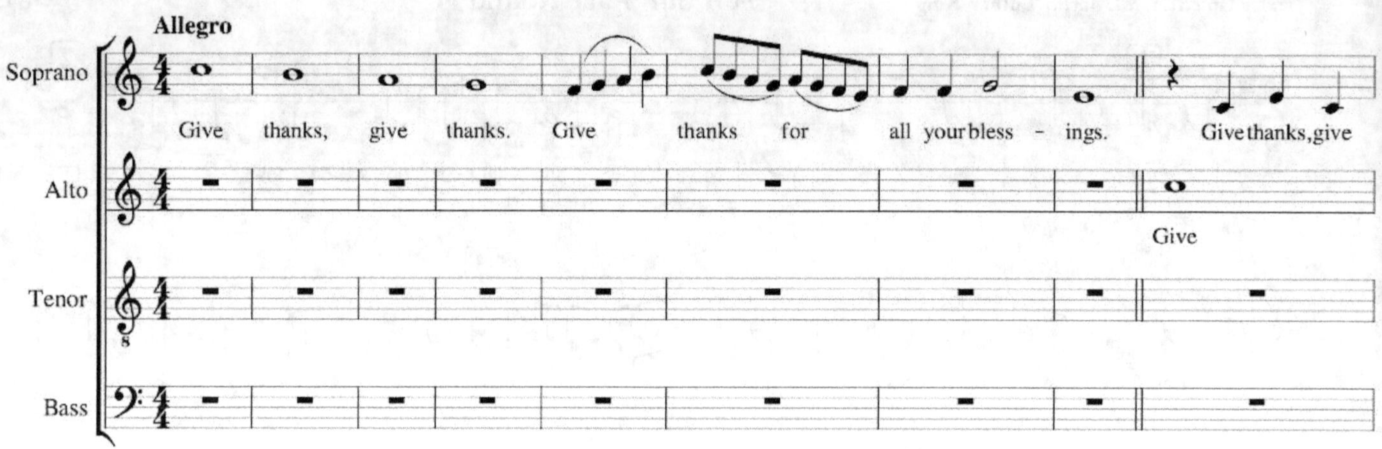

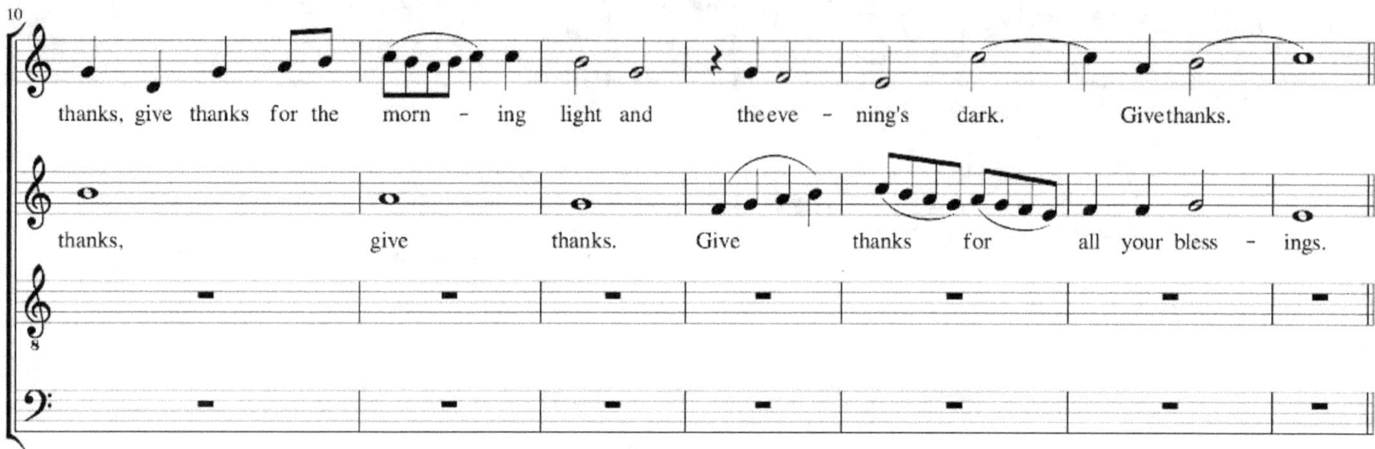

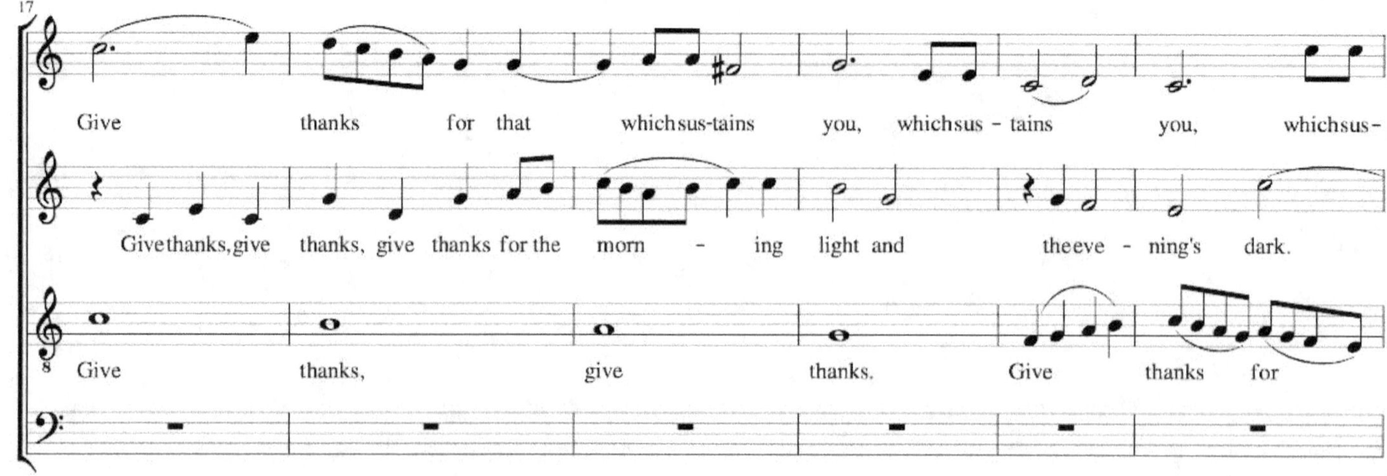

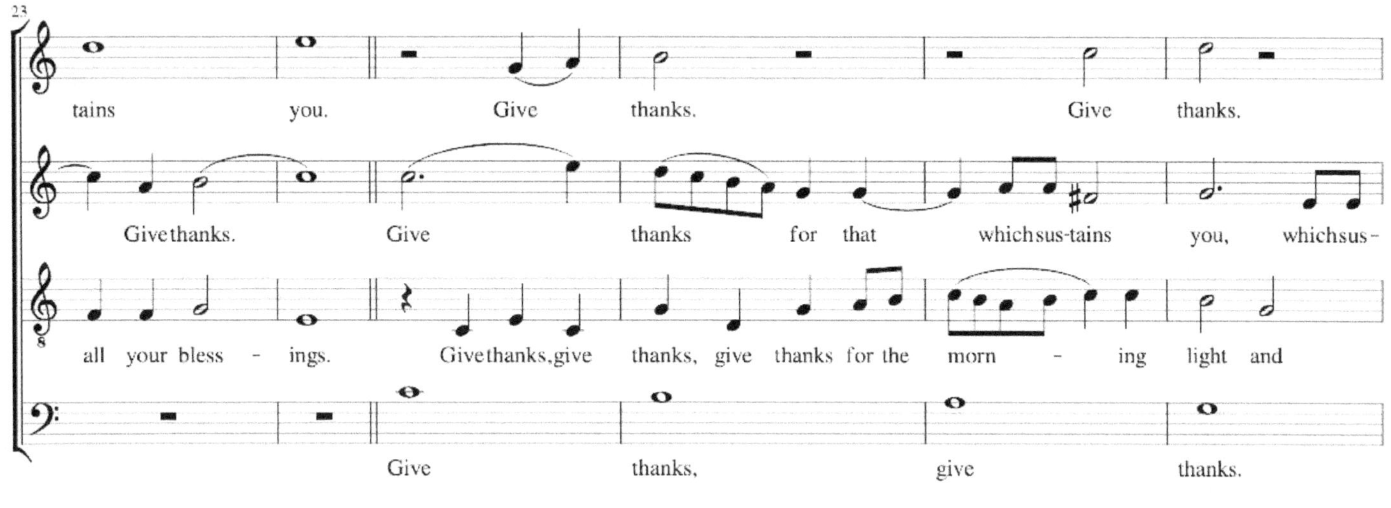
23
tains you. Give thanks. Give thanks.
Give thanks. Give thanks for that which sus-tains you, which sus-
all your bless - ings. Give thanks, give thanks, give thanks for the morn - ing light and
Give thanks, give thanks.

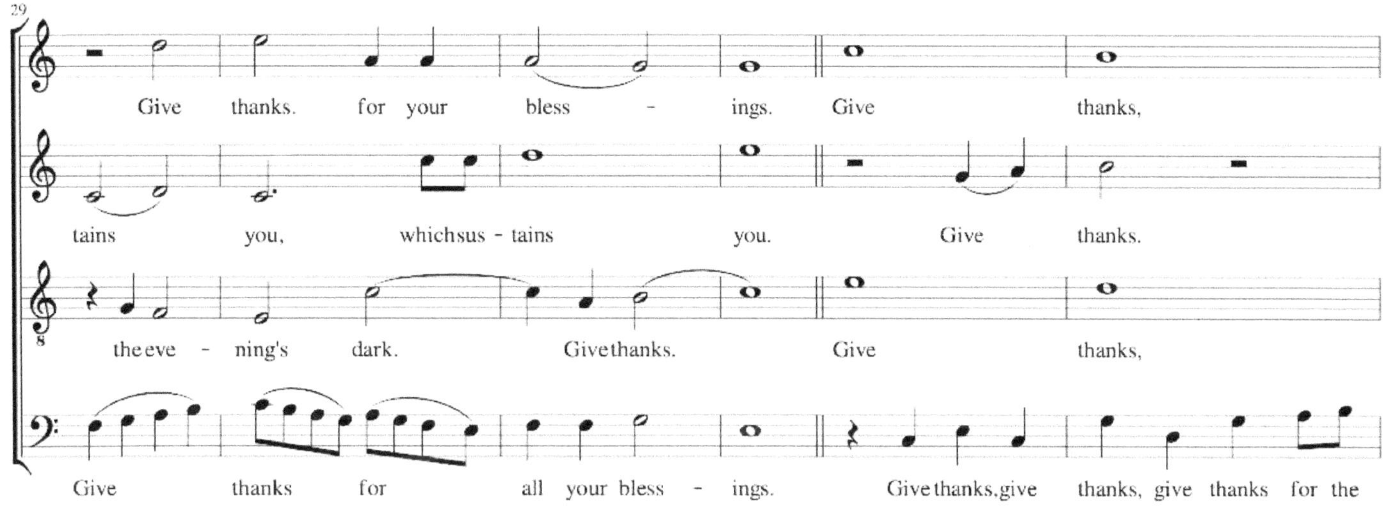
29
Give thanks. for your bless - ings. Give thanks,
tains you, which sus - tains you. Give thanks.
the eve - ning's dark. Give thanks. Give thanks,
Give thanks for all your bless - ings. Give thanks, give thanks, give thanks for the

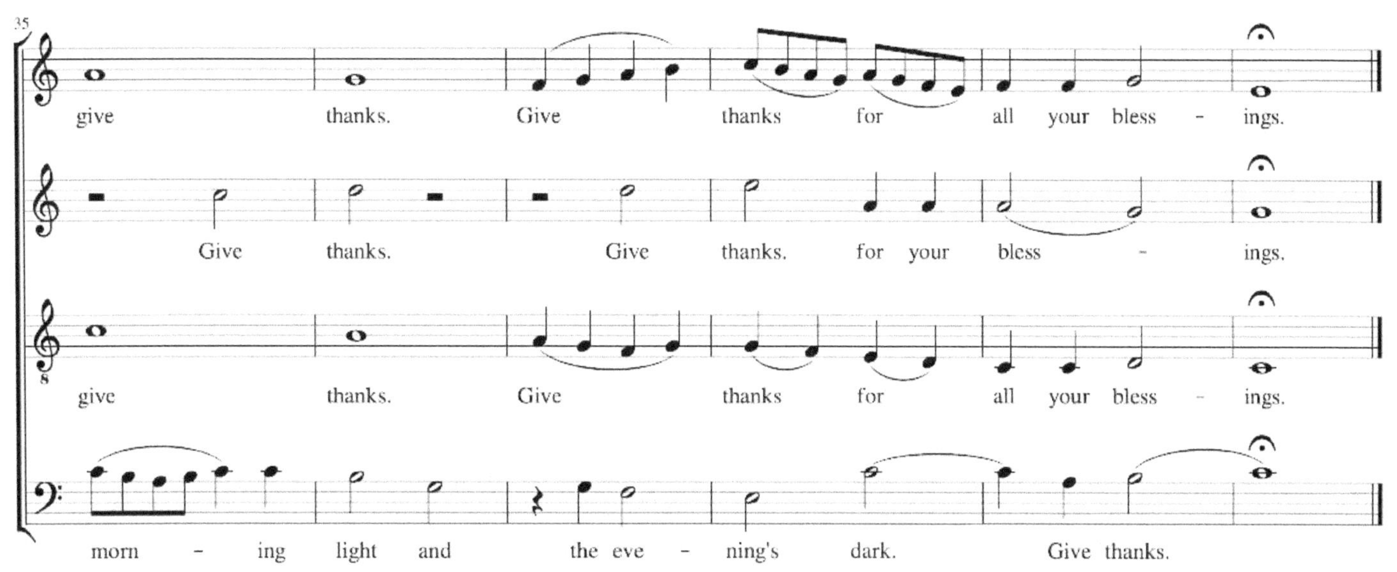
35
give thanks. Give thanks for all your bless - ings.
Give thanks. Give thanks. for your bless - ings.
give thanks. Give thanks for all your bless - ings.
morn - ing light and the eve - ning's dark. Give thanks.

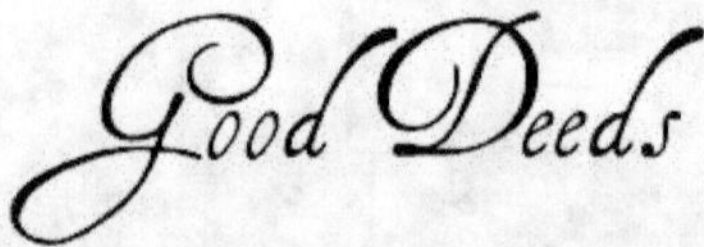

text adapted from Saint Basil
music adapted from Hans Leo Hassler

A Four Part Canon

Ken Langer

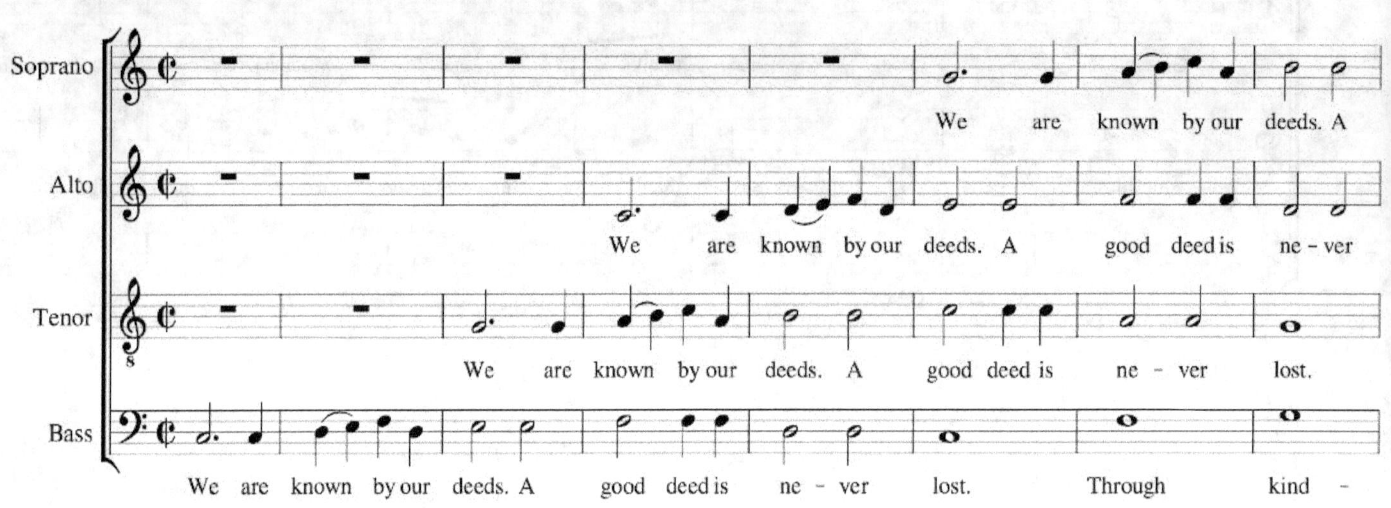

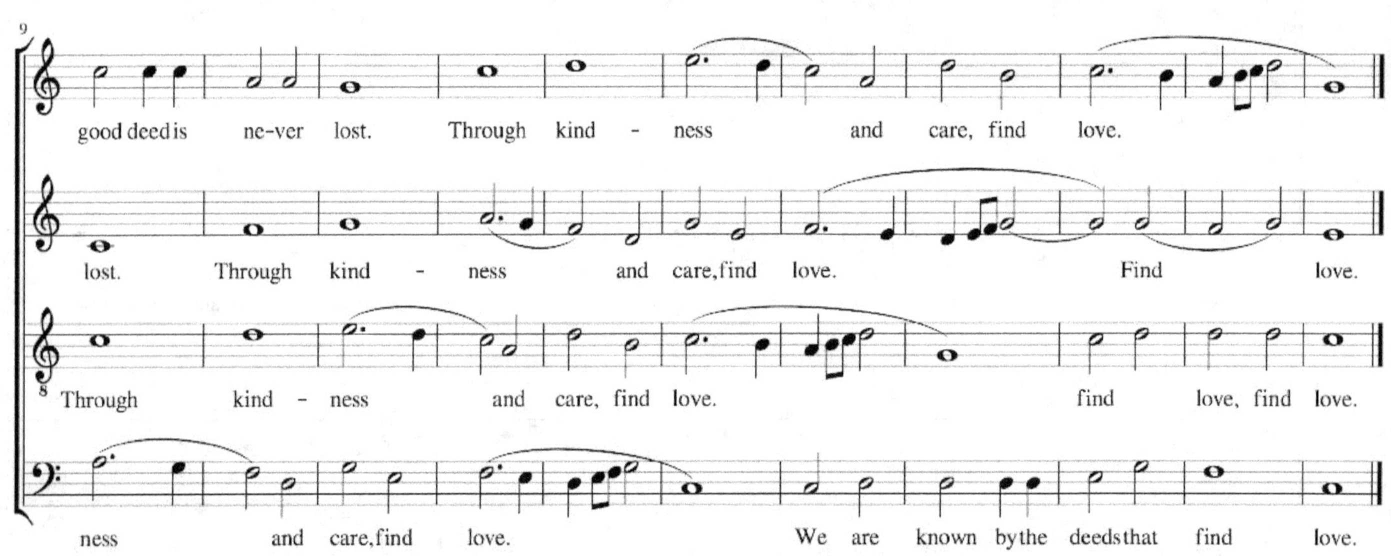

A tree is known by its fruit; a man by his deeds. A good deed is never lost; he who sows courtesy reaps friendship, and he who plants kindness gathers love. ~ Saint Basil

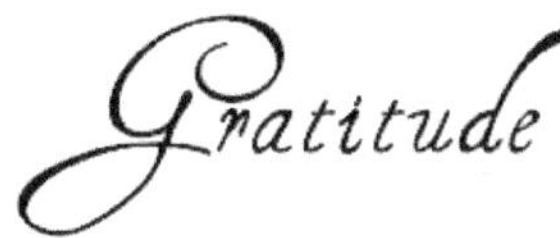

music adapted from Mozart
original text

A Four Part Double Canon

Ken Langer

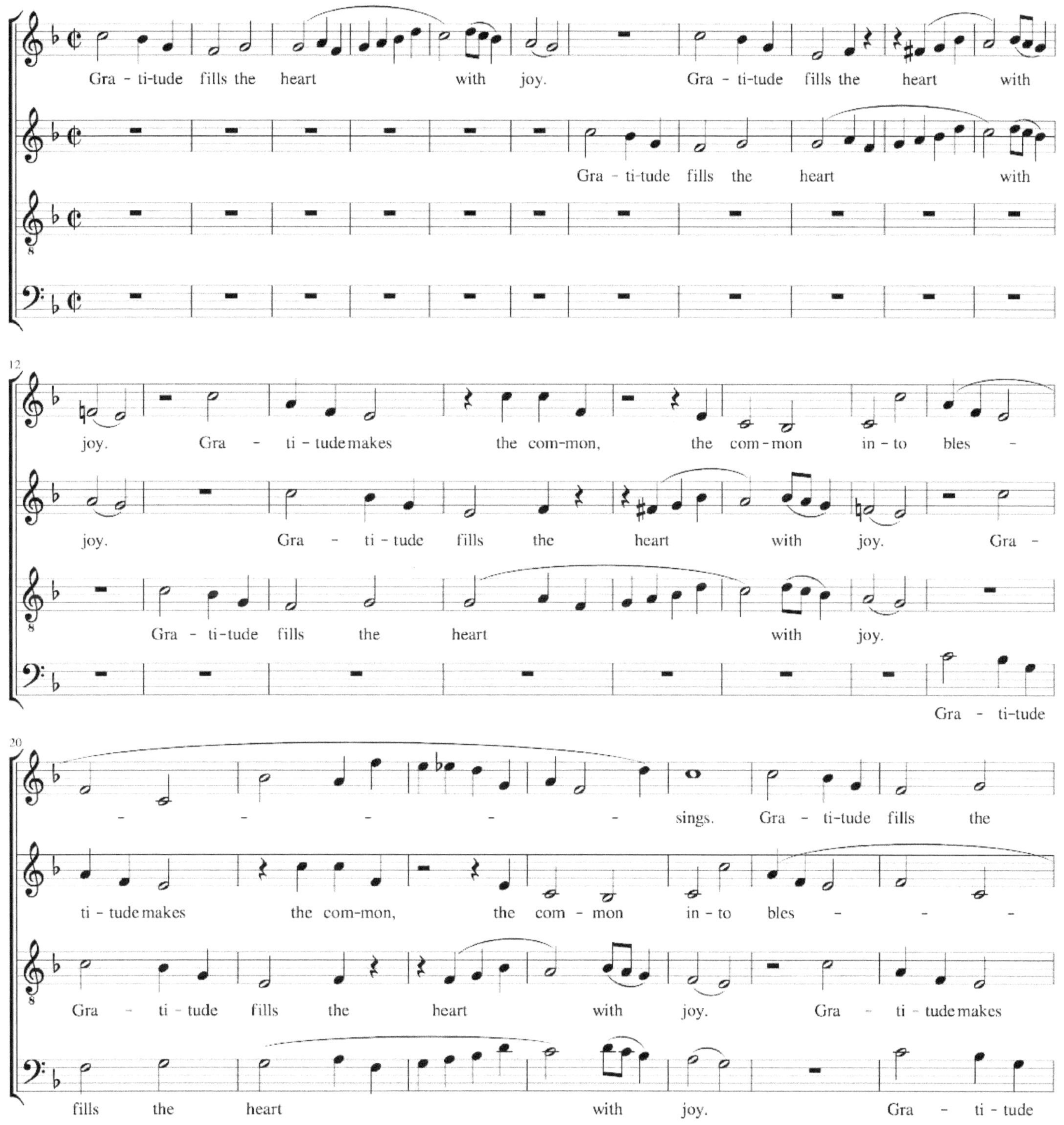

Gra - ti-tude fills the heart with joy. Gra - ti-tude fills the heart with

Gra - ti-tude fills the heart with

12

joy. Gra - ti - tude makes the com-mon, the com - mon in - to bles -

joy. Gra - ti - tude fills the heart with joy. Gra -

Gra - ti-tude fills the heart with joy.

Gra - ti-tude

20

- - - - - sings. Gra - ti-tude fills the

ti - tude makes the com-mon, the com - mon in - to bles - - -

Gra - ti - tude fills the heart with joy. Gra - ti - tude makes

fills the heart with joy. Gra - ti - tude

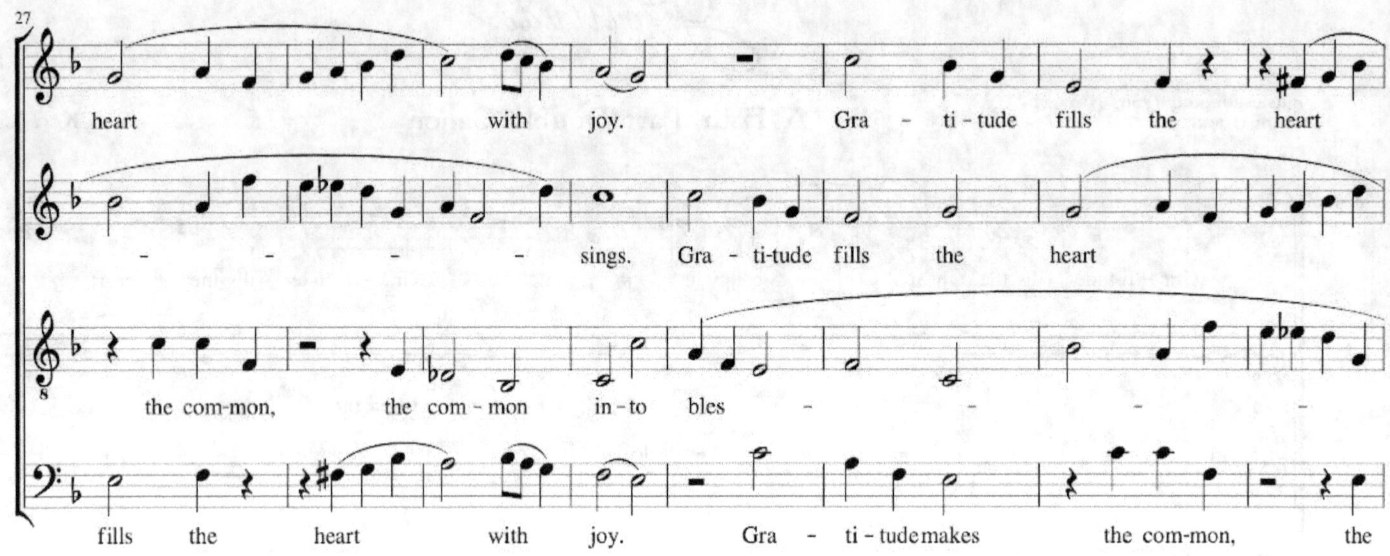
27
heart with joy. Gra - ti - tude fills the heart
- - - - sings. Gra - ti-tude fills the heart
the com-mon, the com - mon in - to bles - - - -
fills the heart with joy. Gra - ti - tude makes the com-mon, the

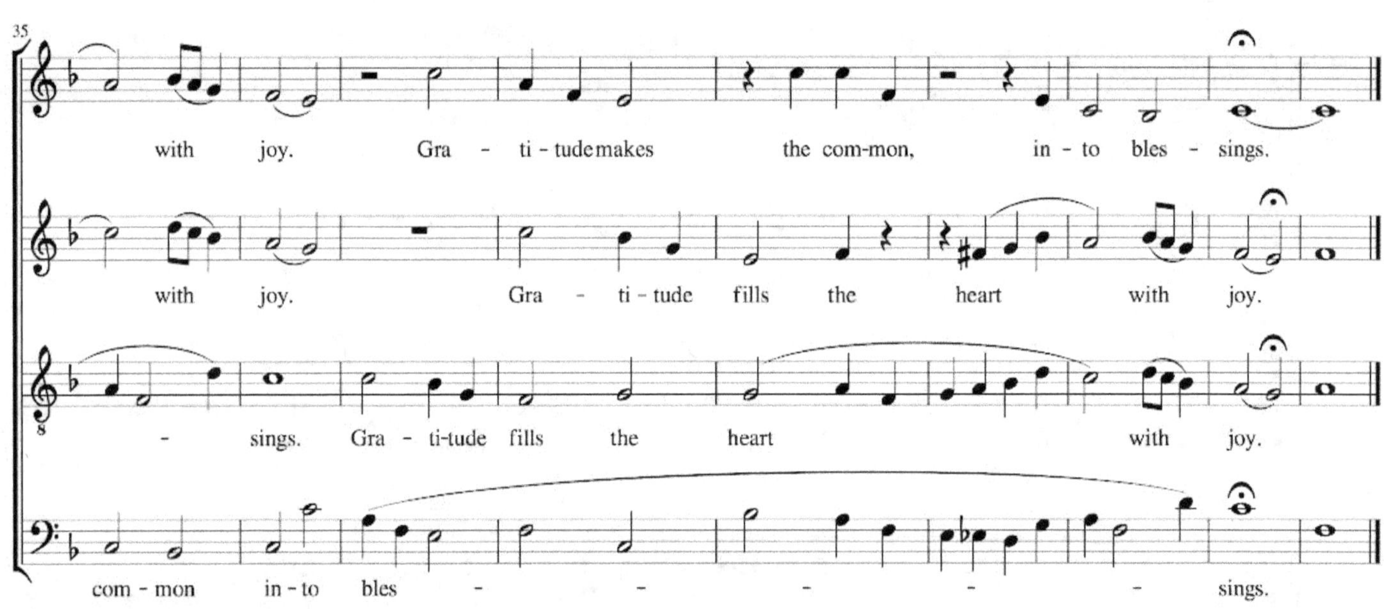
35
with joy. Gra - ti - tude makes the com-mon, in - to bles - sings.
with joy. Gra - ti - tude fills the heart with joy.
- sings. Gra - ti-tude fills the heart with joy.
com - mon in - to bles - - - - - sings.

Happiness

original music
text adapted from the Dalai Lama

A Four Part Canon

Ken Langer

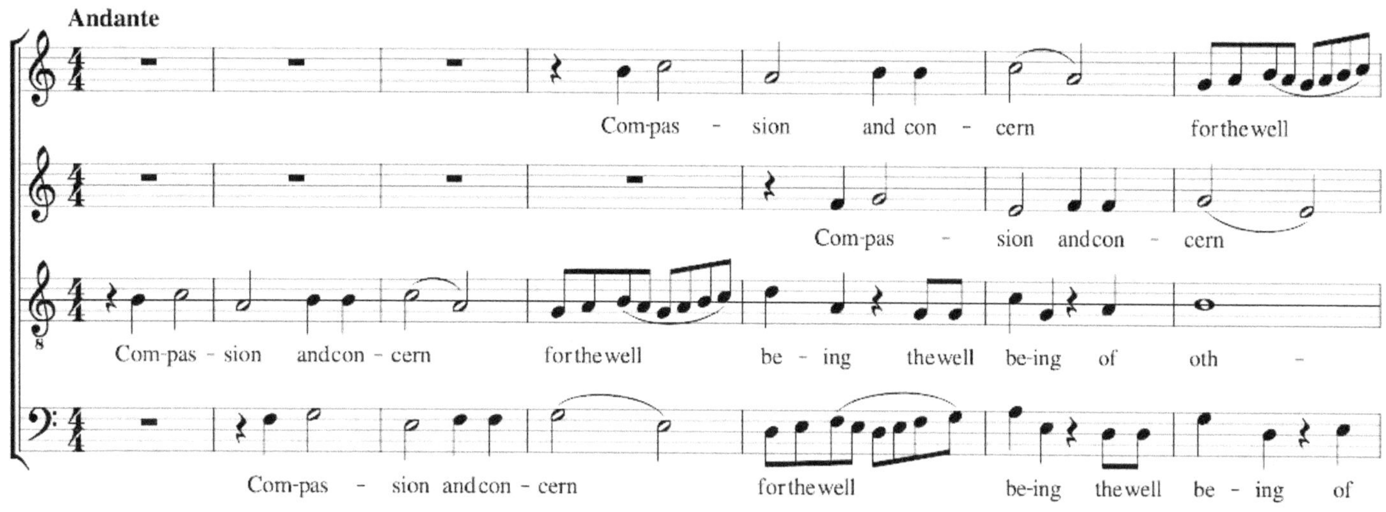

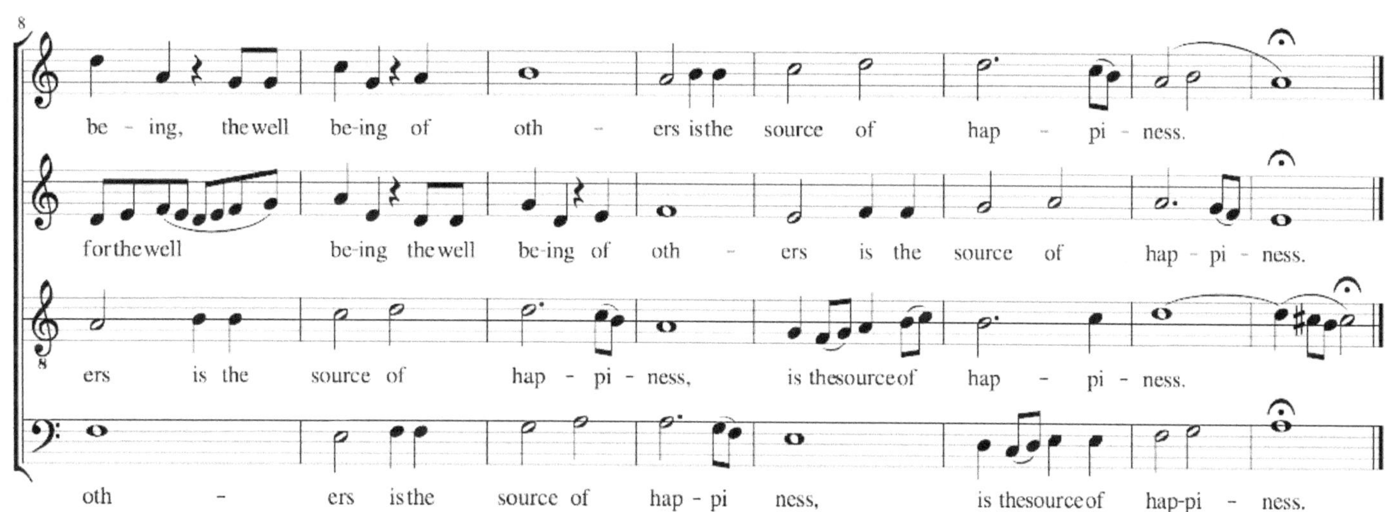

A compassionate mind, a sense of concern for the well being of others.
This is the source of happiness. ~ the Dalai Lama

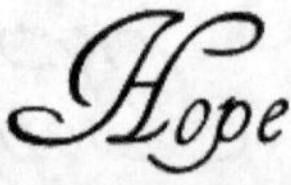

A Three Part Canon

music adapted from Praetorius
text adapted from Martin Luther King

Ken Langer

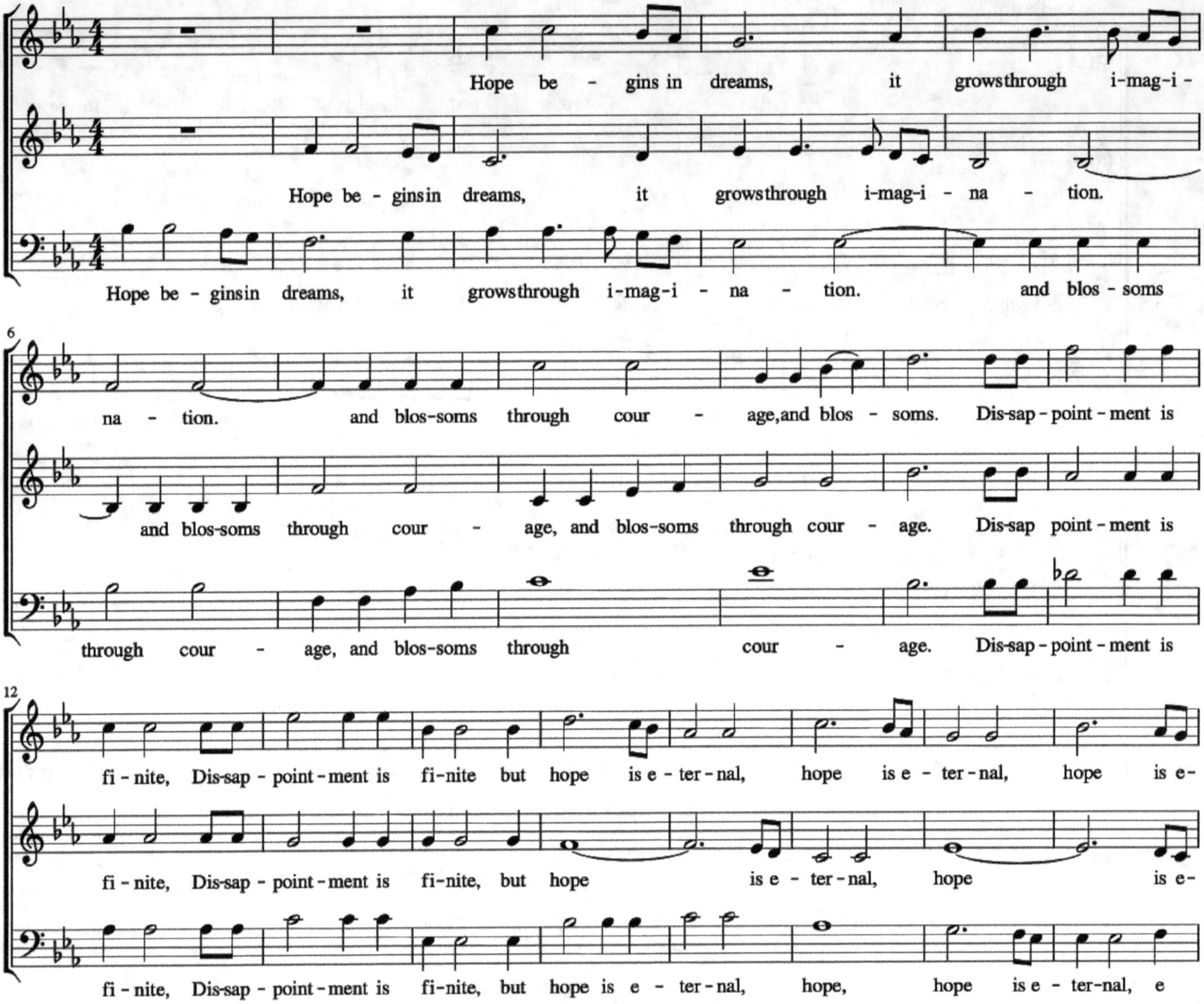

Hope be - gins in dreams, it grows through i-mag-i -
Hope be - gins in dreams, it grows through i-mag-i - na - tion.
Hope be - gins in dreams, it grows through i-mag-i - na - tion. and blos - soms

6
na - tion. and blos-soms through cour - age, and blos - soms. Dis-sap - point - ment is
and blos-soms through cour - age, and blos-soms through cour - age. Dis-sap point - ment is
through cour - age, and blos-soms through cour - age. Dis-sap - point - ment is

12
fi - nite, Dis-sap - point - ment is fi-nite but hope is e - ter - nal, hope is e - ter - nal, hope is e-
fi - nite, Dis-sap - point - ment is fi-nite, but hope is e - ter - nal, hope is e-
fi - nite, Dis-sap - point - ment is fi-nite, but hope is e - ter - nal, hope, hope is e - ter-nal, e

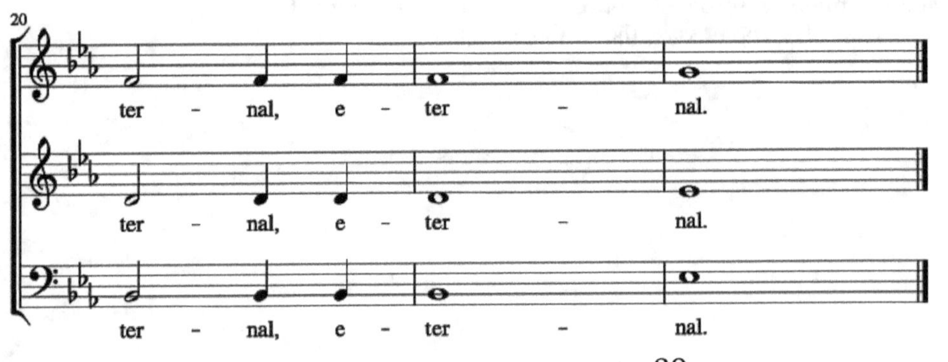

We must accept finite disappointment, but never lose infinite hope.
~ Martin Luther King, Jr.

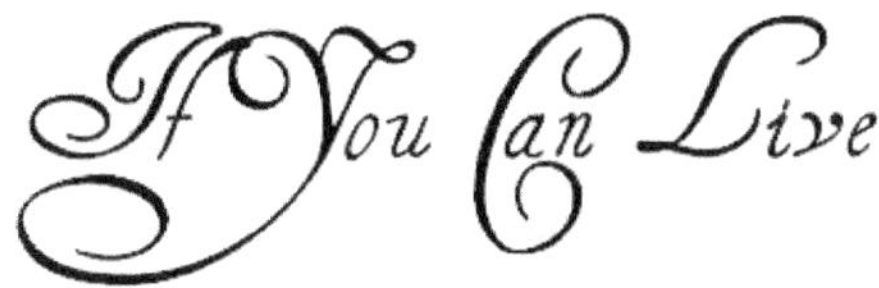

original music
original text

A Four Part Augmentation Canon

Ken Langer

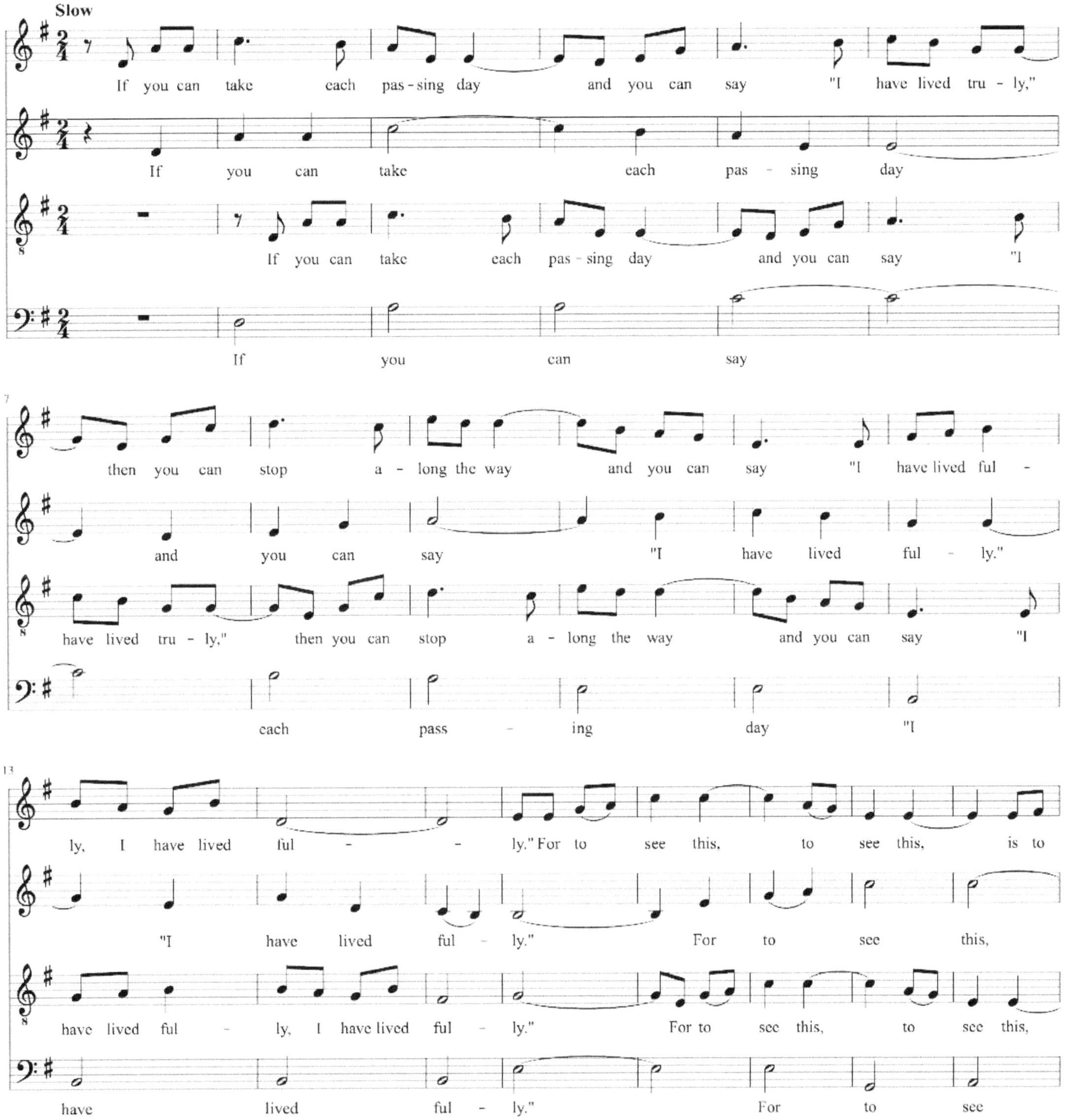

Slow

If you can take each pas - sing day and you can say "I have lived tru - ly,"

If you can take each pas - sing day

If you can take each pas - sing day and you can say "I

If you can say

7

then you can stop a - long the way and you can say "I have lived ful -

and you can say "I have lived ful - ly."

have lived tru - ly," then you can stop a - long the way and you can say "I

each pass - ing day "I

13

ly, I have lived ful - - ly." For to see this, to see this, is to

"I have lived ful - ly." For to see this,

have lived ful - ly, I have lived ful - ly." For to see this, to see this,

have lived ful - ly." For to see

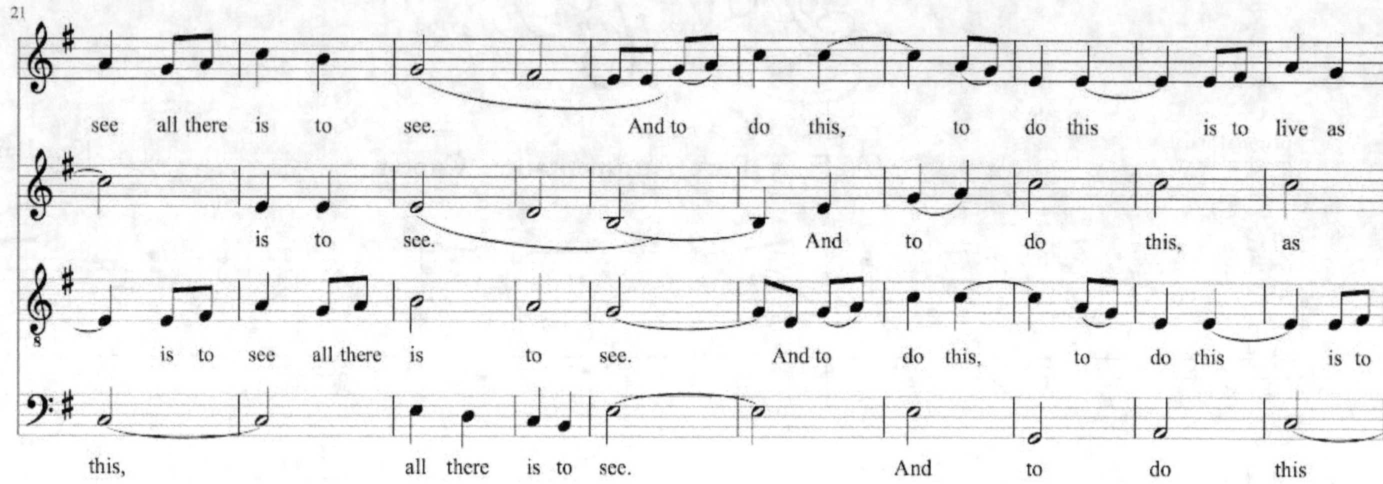
21
see all there is to see. And to do this, to do this is to live as
is to see. And to do this, as
is to see all there is to see. And to do this, to do this is to
this, all there is to see. And to do this

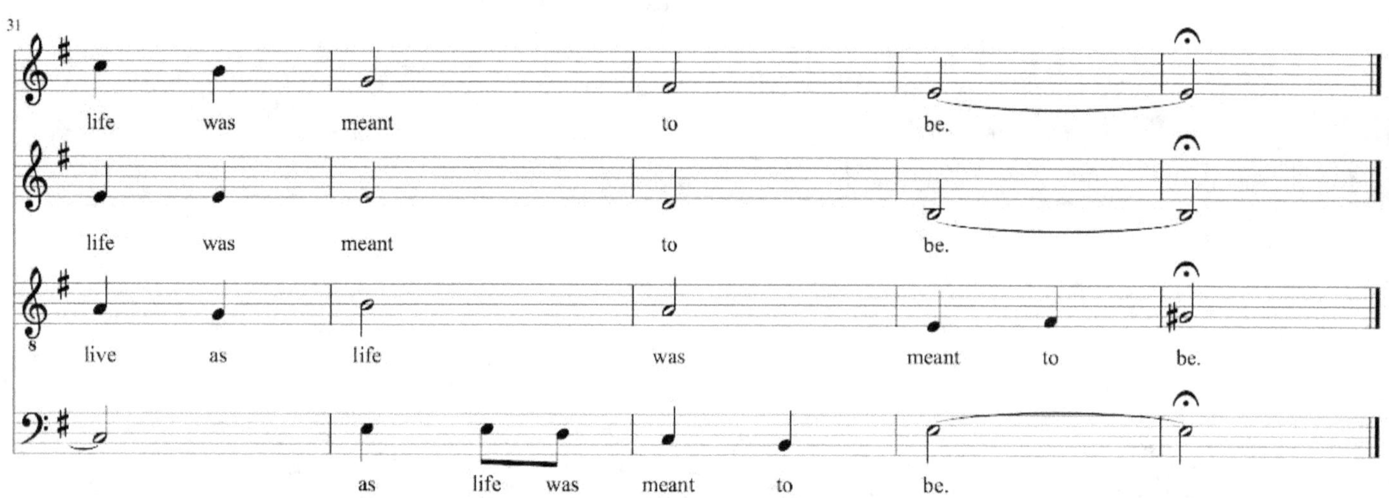
31
life was meant to be.
life was meant to be.
live as life was meant to be.
as life was meant to be.

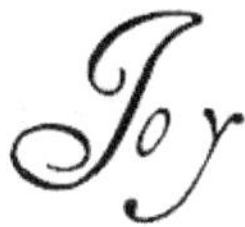

music adapted from Antonio Caldera
text adapted from Mother Theresa

A Three Part Round

Ken Langer

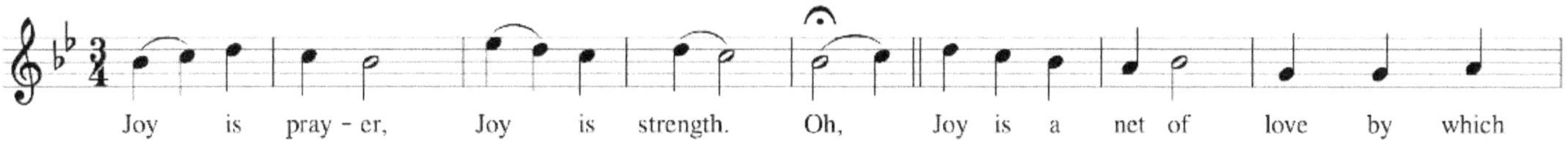

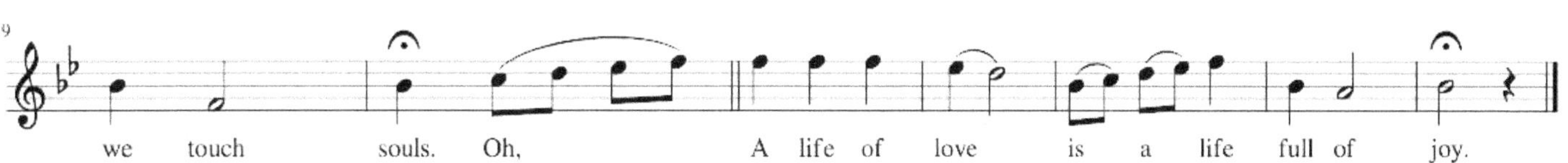

Joy is prayer; joy is strength: joy is love; joy is a net of love by which you can catch souls. ˜ Mother Theresa

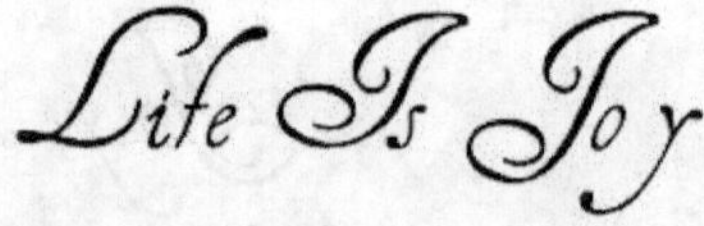

original music
original text

A Four Part Canon

Ken Langer

Lively

Moderate

Life is joy! Life is sor-row. Life is joy! Life is sor-row. Life is joy! Life is sor-row. for they are

Life is joy! Life is sor-row. Life is joy! Life is sor-row. Life is joy! Life is sor-row.

Life is joy! Life is sor-row. Life is joy! Life is sor - row. Life is joy!

Life is joy! Life is sor-row. Life is joy! Life is sor - row.

9

part of the same truth. truth. So, seek the joy, the joy

for they are part of the same truth. truth. truth. seek the

Life is sor-row. for they are part of the same truth. truth.

Life is joy! Life is sor-row. for they are part of the same truth.

17

and ac-cept the sor - row, ac - cept the sor - ow. Life shall be, life shall be, life shall be

joy, the joy and ac-cept the sor - row, ac - cept the sor - row. Life shall be, life shall be,

seek the joy, the joy and ac-cept the sor - row, ac - cept the sor - row. Life shall be,

seek the joy, the joy and ac-cept the sor-row, sor - row.

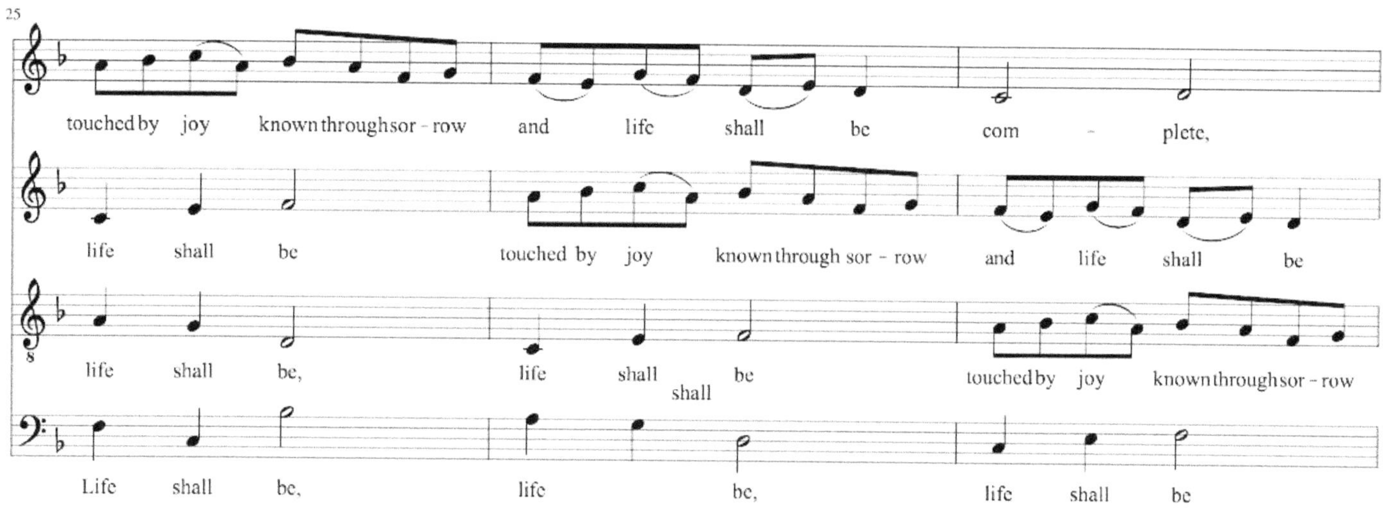
25
touched by joy known through sor - row and life shall be com - plete,
life shall be touched by joy known through sor - row and life shall be
life shall be, life shall shall be touched by joy known through sor - row
Life shall be, life be, life shall be

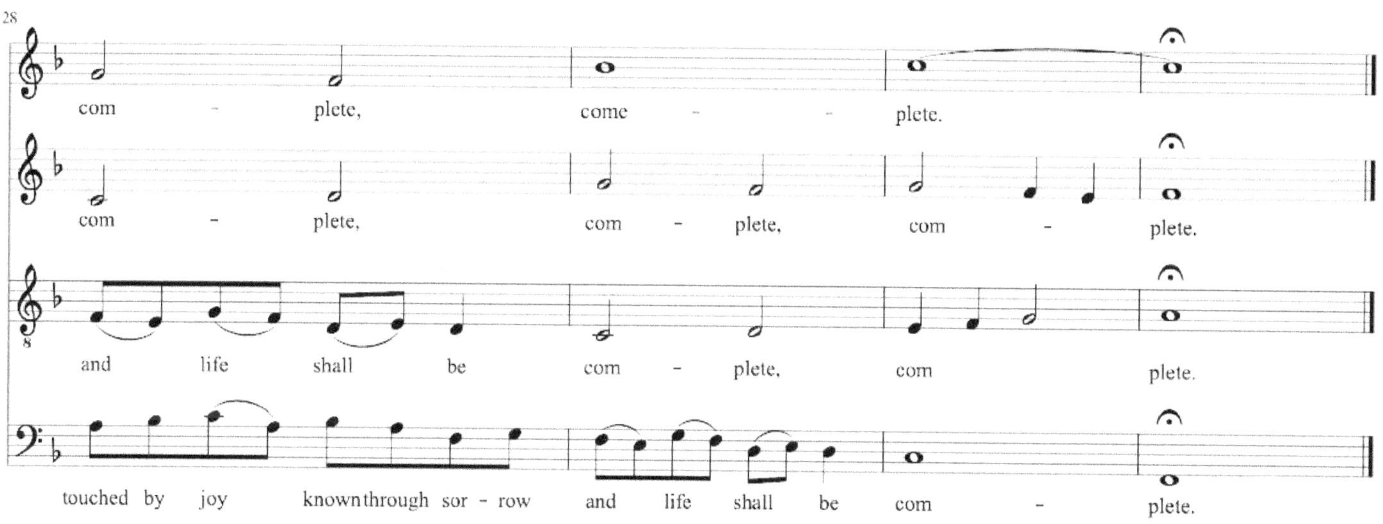
28
com - plete, come - - plete.
com - plete, com - plete, com - plete.
and life shall be com - plete, com plete.
touched by joy known through sor - row and life shall be com - plete.

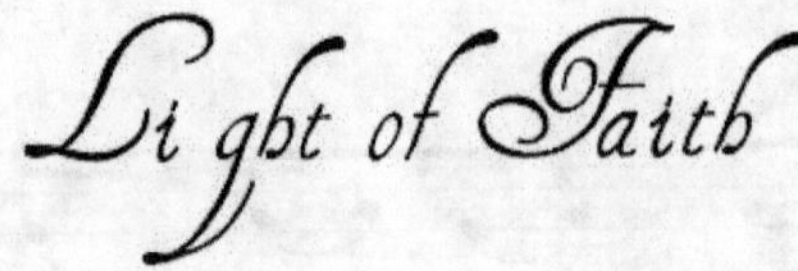

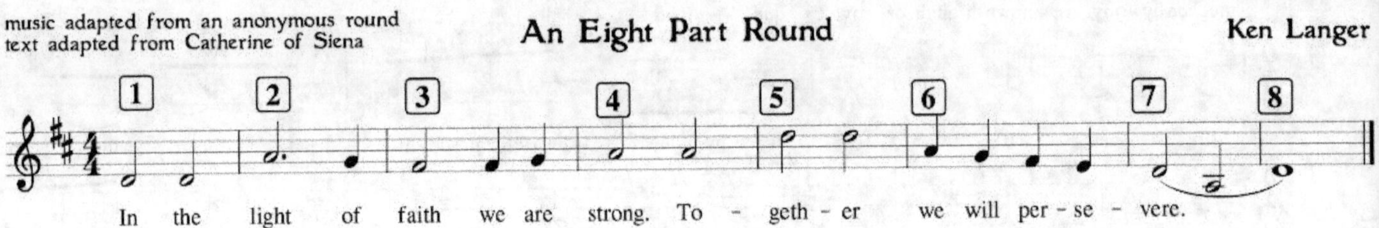

In the light of faith I am strong, constant, and persevering. ~ Catherine of Siena

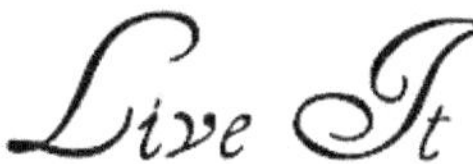

text adapted from Sai Baba
music adapted from Mozart

A Four Part Round With Coda

Ken Langer

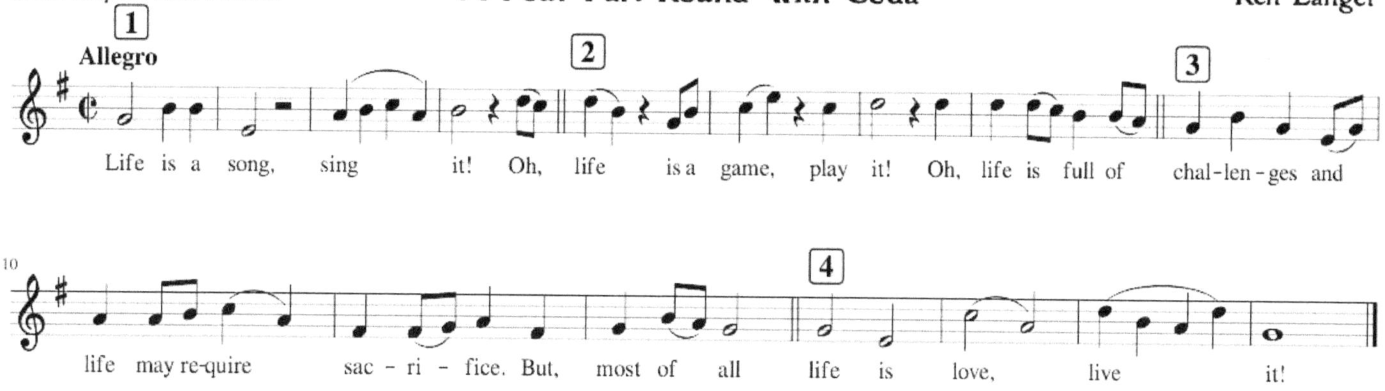

1 Allegro

Life is a song, sing it! Oh, 2 life is a game, play it! Oh, life is full of 3 chal-len-ges and life may re-quire sac - ri - fice. But, most of all 4 life is love, live it!

Optional Coda:

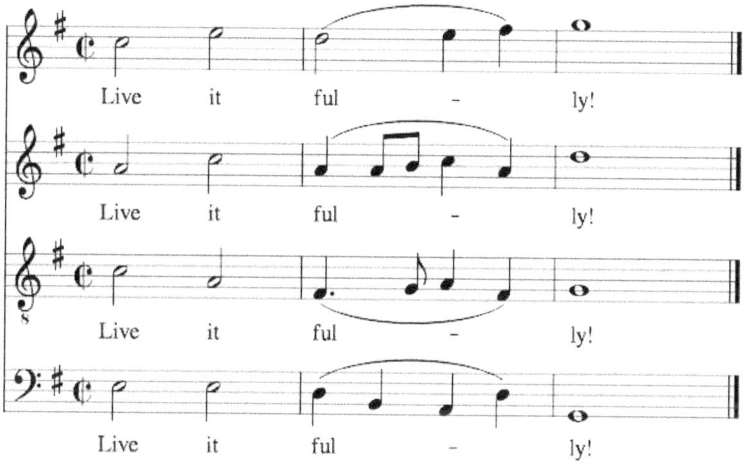

Live it ful - ly!

Live it ful - ly!

Live it ful - ly!

Live it ful - ly!

Life is a song - sing it. Life is a game - play it. Life is a challenge - meet it.
Life is a dream - realize it. Life is a sacrifice - offer it. Life is love - enjoy it. ~ Sai Baba

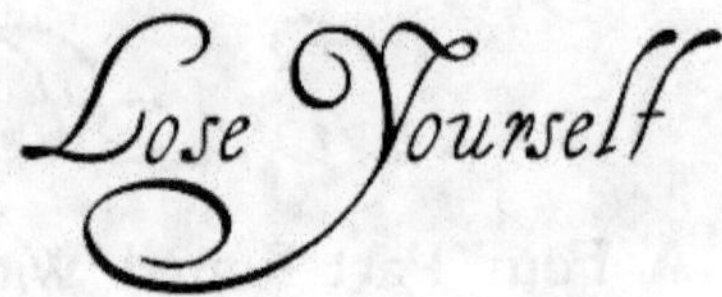

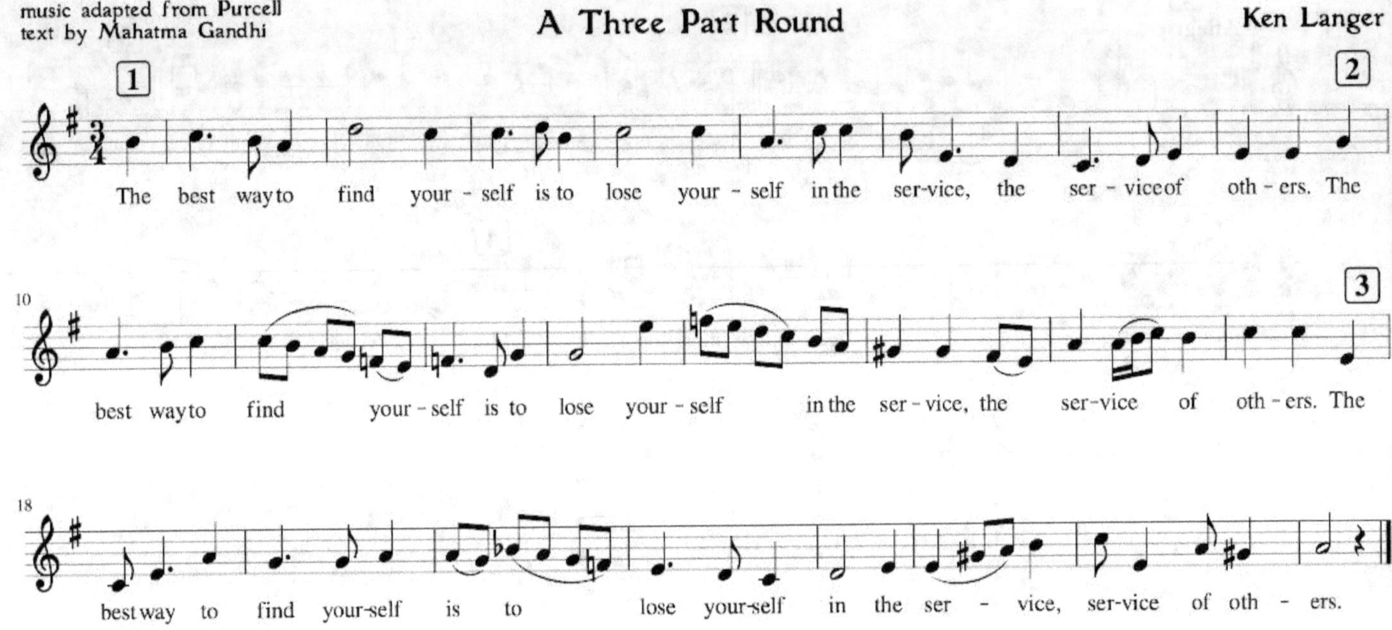

The best way to find yourself is to lose yourself in the service of others ~ Mahatma Gandhi

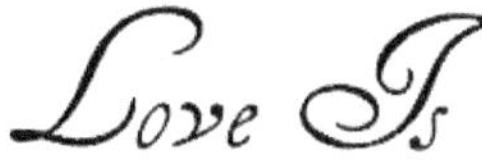

A Four Part Canon

music adapted from John Callcott
text adapted from Robert Fulghum

Ken Langer

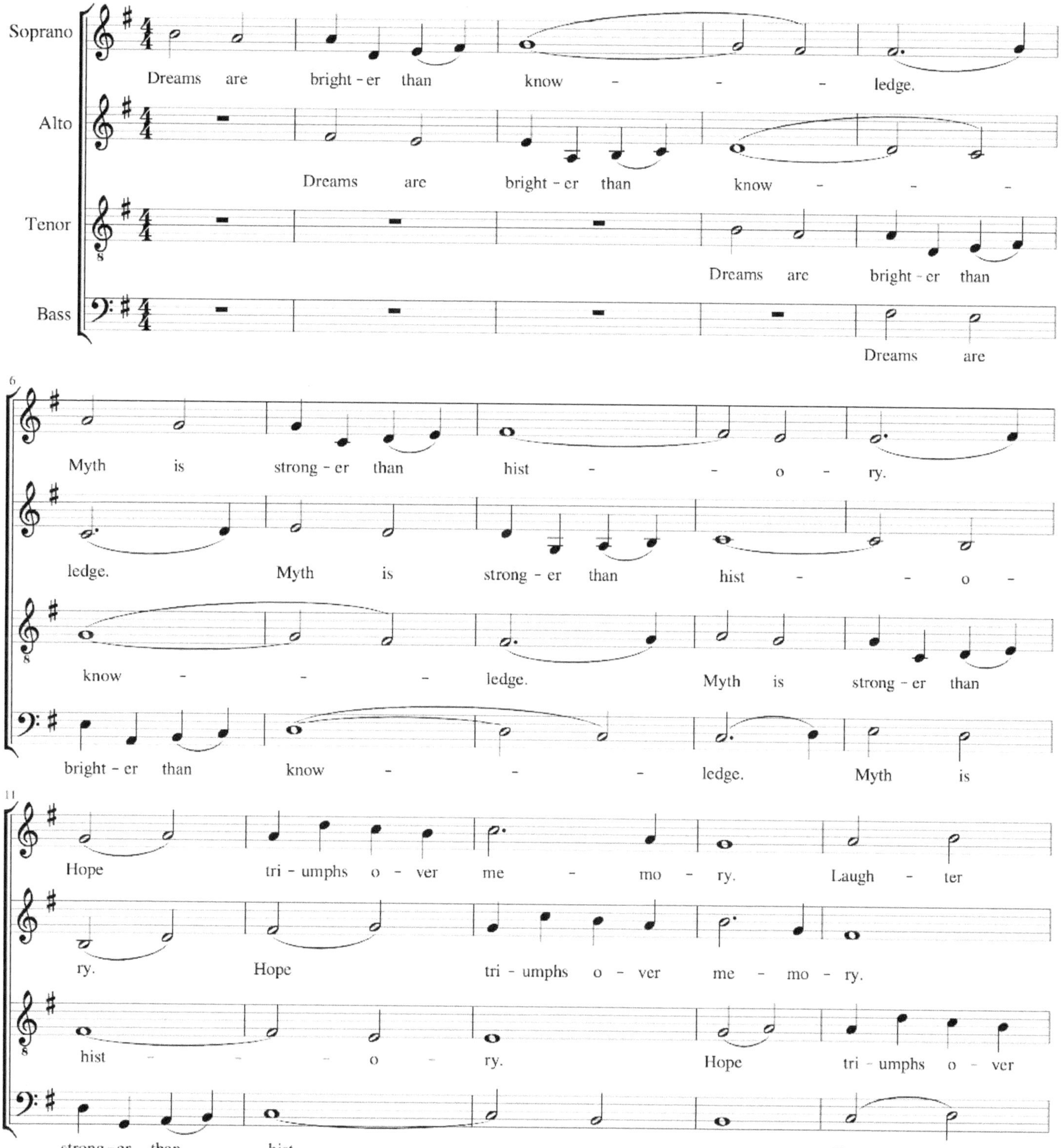

Soprano
Dreams are bright - er than know - - - ledge.

Alto
Dreams are bright - er than know - - -

Tenor
Dreams are bright - er than

Bass
Dreams are

Myth is strong - er than hist - - o - ry.

ledge. Myth is strong - er than hist - - o -

know - - - ledge. Myth is strong - er than

bright - er than know - - - ledge. Myth is

Hope tri - umphs o - ver me - mo - ry. Laugh - ter

ry. Hope tri - umphs o - ver me - mo - ry.

hist - - - o - ry. Hope tri - umphs o - ver

strong - er than hist - - - o - ry. Hope

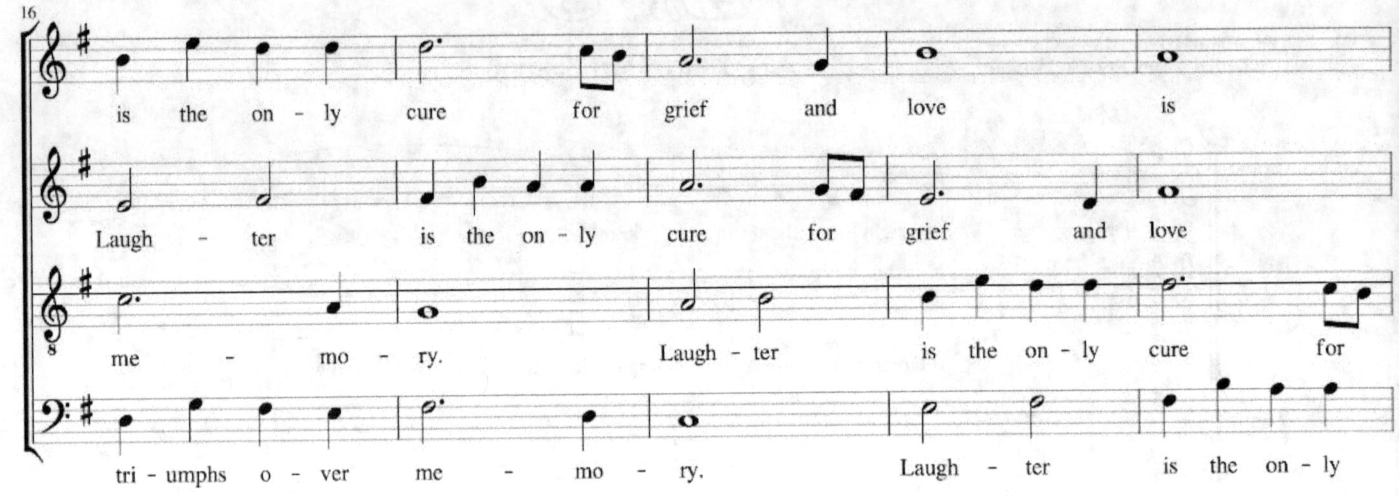

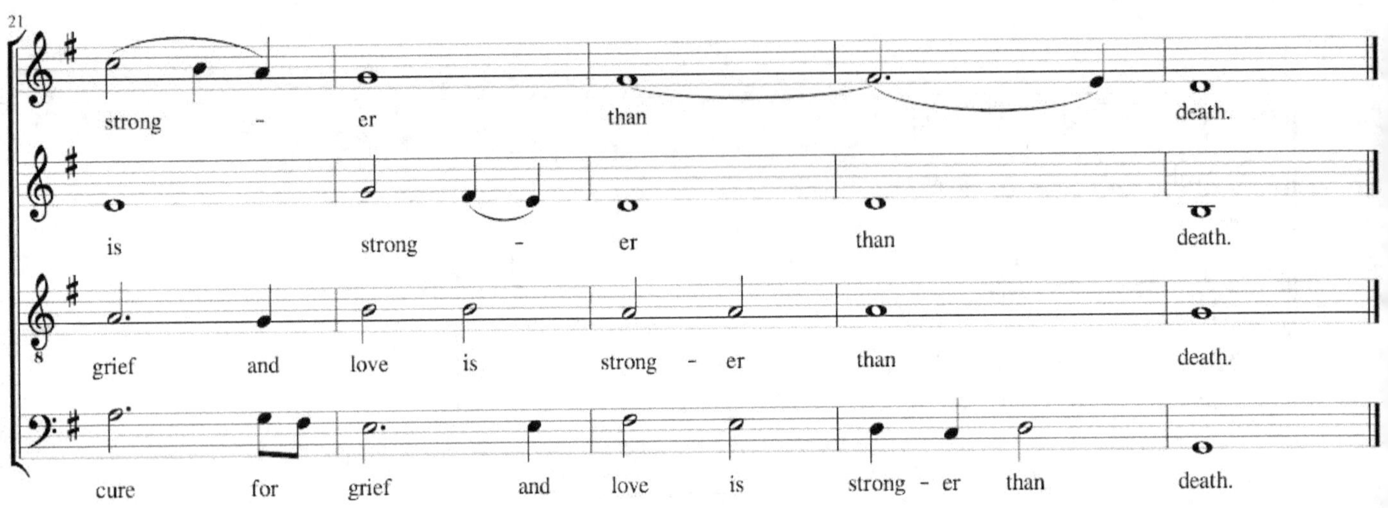

I believe that imagination is stronger than knowledge. That myth is more potent than history.
That dreams are more powerful than facts. That hope always triumphs over experience.
That laughter is the only cure for grief. And I believe that love is stronger than death. ~ Robert Fulghum

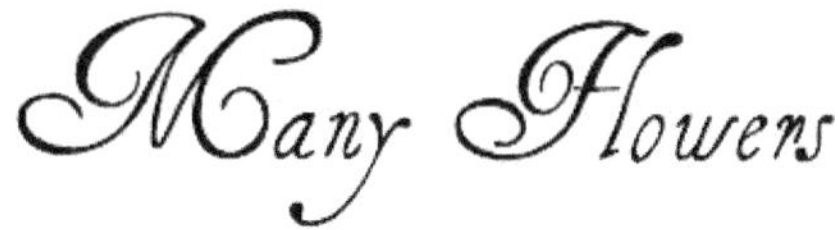

original music
original text

A Four Part Round

Ken Langer

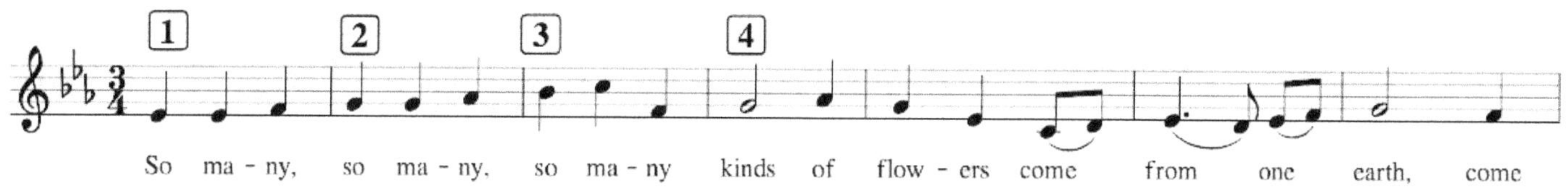

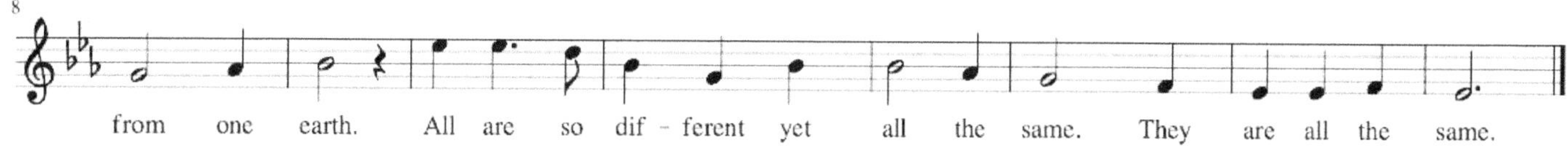

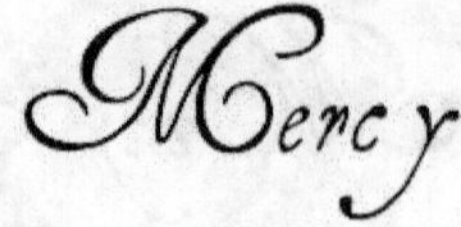

text adapted from Chanakya
original music

A Three Part Round

Ken Langer

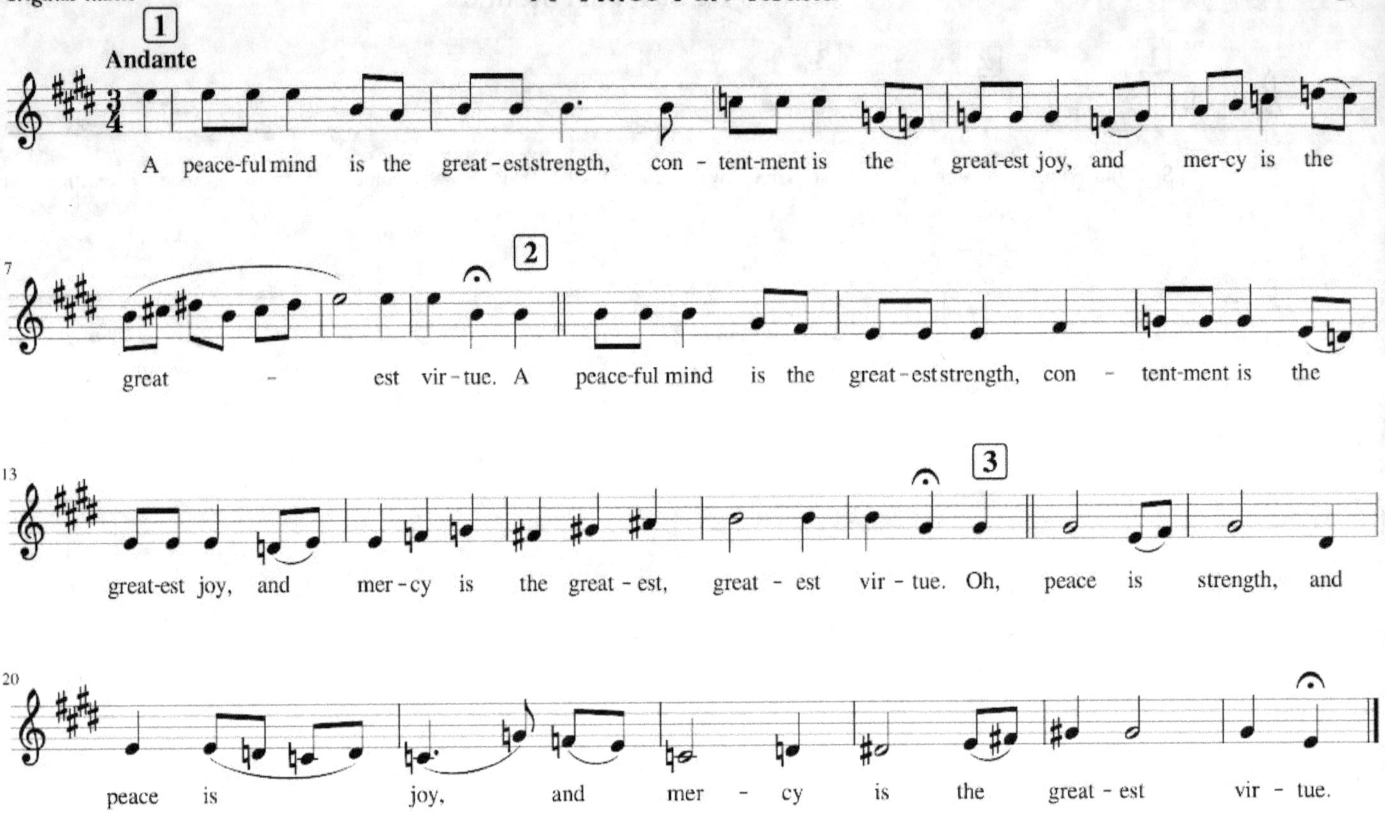

1
Andante

A peace-ful mind is the great - est strength, con - tent-ment is the great-est joy, and mer-cy is the

7 great - est vir - tue. 2 A peace-ful mind is the great - est strength, con - tent-ment is the

13 great-est joy, and mer - cy is the great - est, great - est vir - tue. 3 Oh, peace is strength, and

20 peace is joy, and mer - cy is the great - est vir - tue.

There is no austerity equal to a balanced mind, and there is no happiness equal to contentment; there is no disease like covetousness, and no virtue like mercy. ~ Chanakya

My Heart Sings

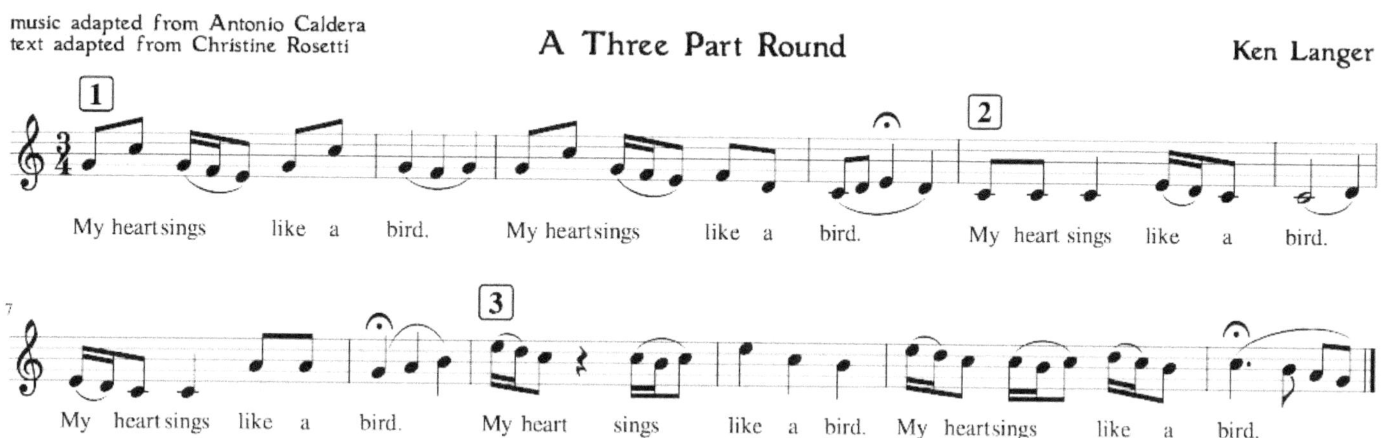

My heart is like a singing bird. ~ Christina Rosetti

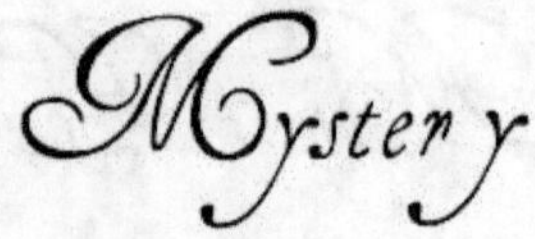
Mystery

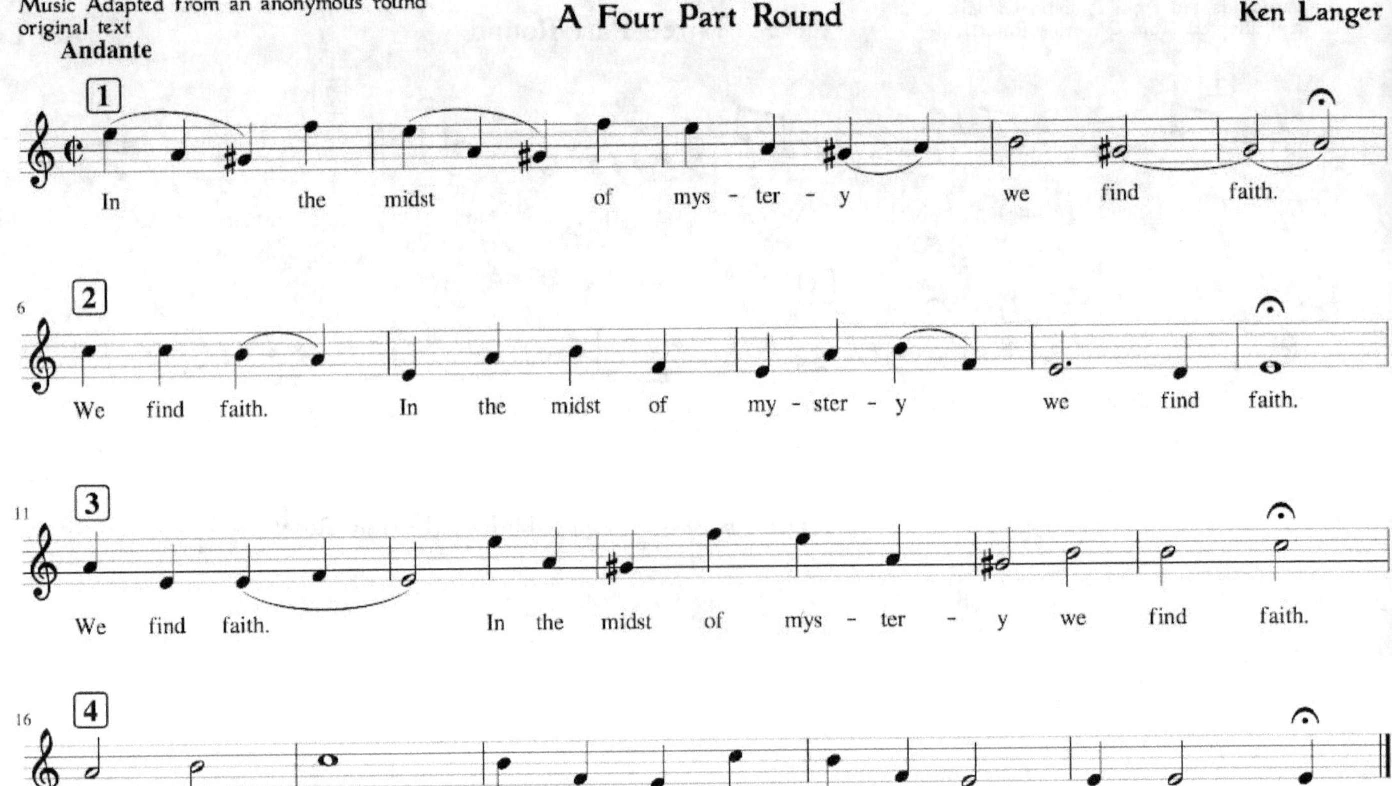
Music Adapted from an anonymous round
original text
A Four Part Round
Ken Langer
Andante
1
In the midst of mys - ter - y we find faith.
2
We find faith. In the midst of my - ster - y we find faith.
3
We find faith. In the midst of mys - ter - y we find faith.
4
We find faith. In the midst of my - ster - y we find faith.

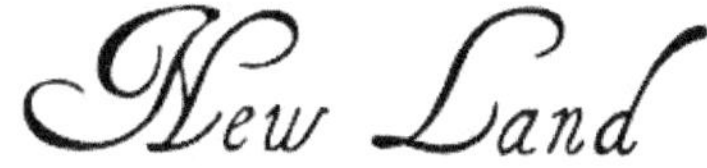

music adapted from Giovanni Bataloni
original text

A Three Part Round

Ken Langer

1
Ours is a jour - ney from birth to death.

5 2
Ours is a chance to ex - plore new lands.

9 3
Each age, each age is a new land to disc - o - ver.

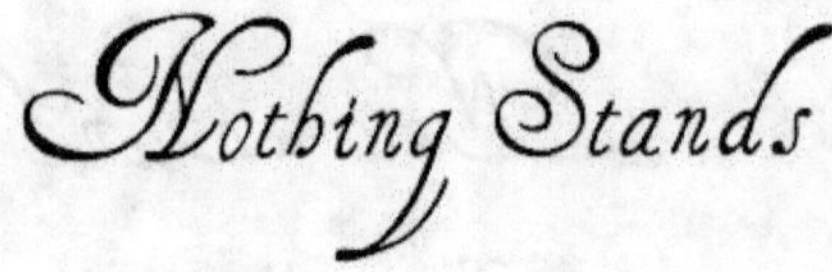

original music
text adapted from Henry David Thoreau

A Three Part Round

Ken Langer

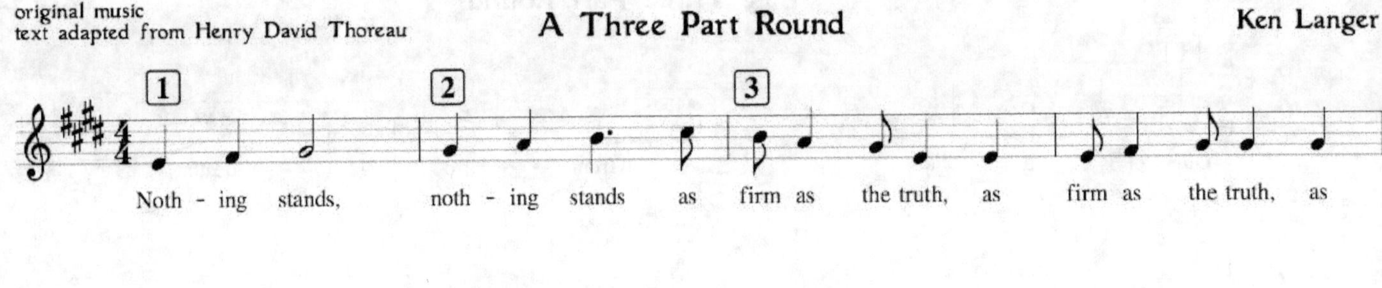

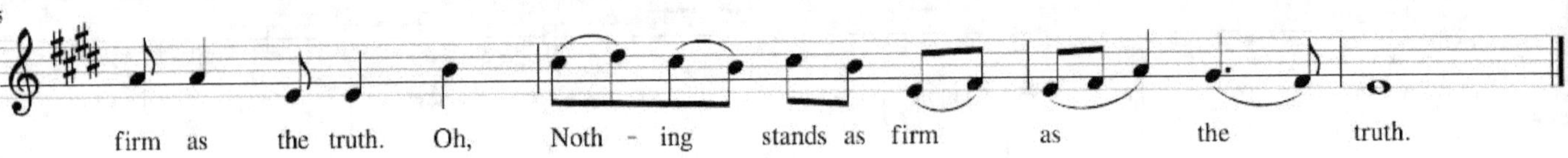

No face which we can give to a matter will stead us so well at last as the truth.
This alone wears well. ~ Henry David Thoreau

One and the Same

music adapted from Antonio Caldera
text adapted from Mahatma Gandhi

A Three Part Round

Ken Langer

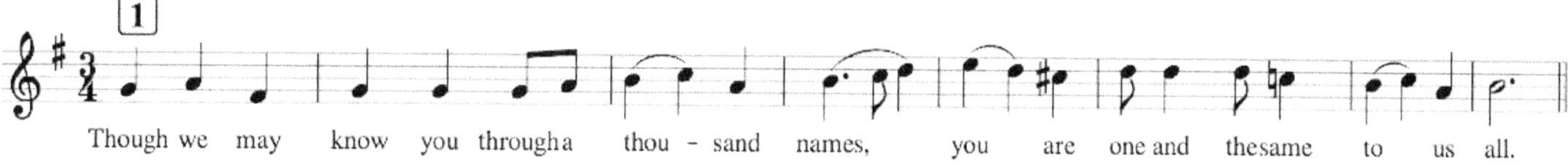

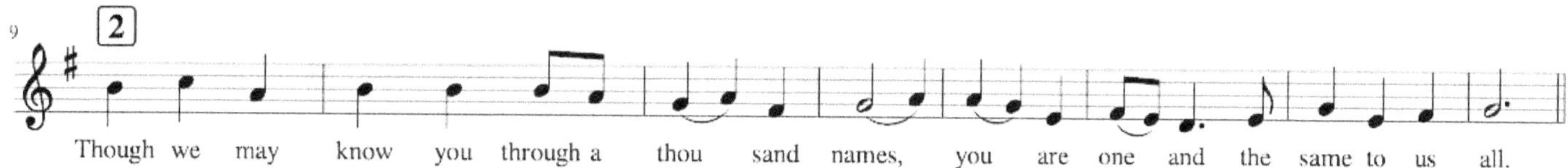

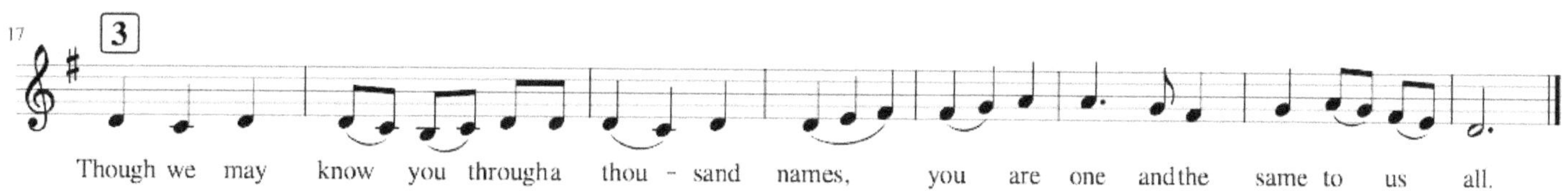

Though we may know Him by a thousand names, He is one and the same to us all. ~ Mahatma Gandhi

Only Good

music adapted from an anonymous round
text by Herodotus

A Three Part Round

Ken Langer

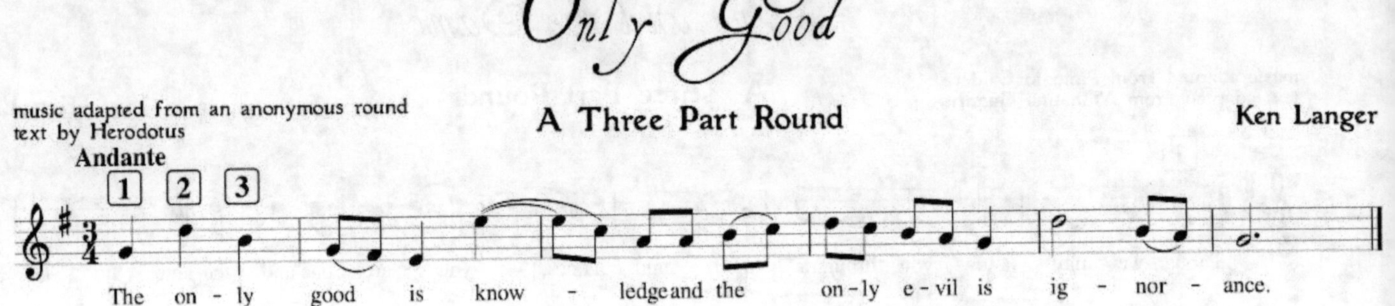

The only good is knowledge, and the only evil is ignorance. ~ Herodotus

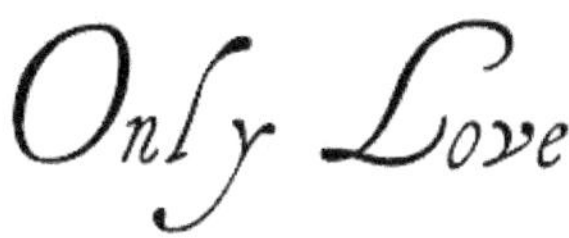

music adapted from a round by
Thomas Ravenscroft
text adapted from Martin Luther King

A Three Part Round

Ken Langer

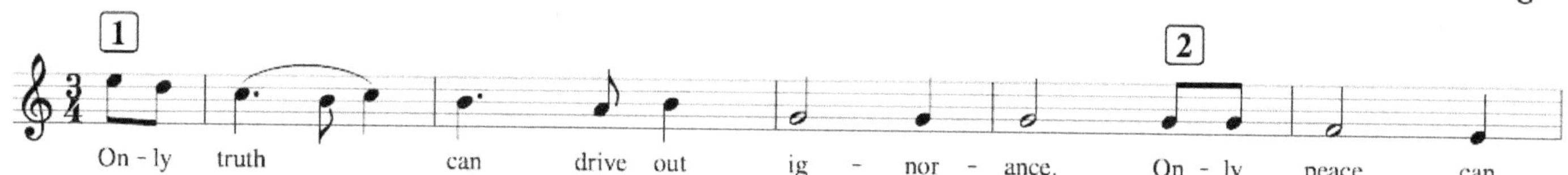

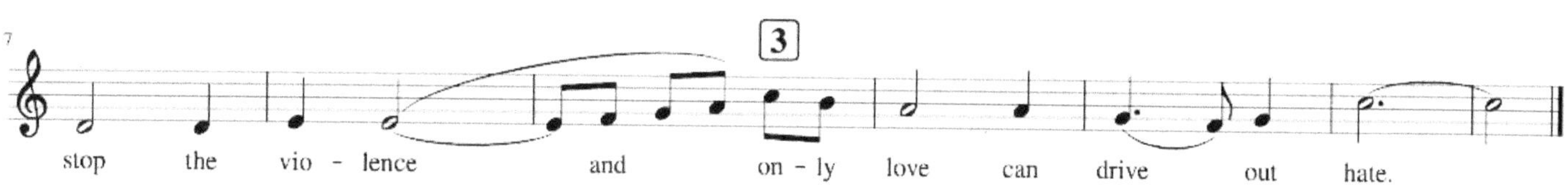

Darkness cannot drive out darkness; only light can do that. Hate cannot drive out hate; only love can do that. ~ Martin Luther King, Jr

Our Promise

A Three Part Canon

music adapted from Beethoven
original text

Ken Langer

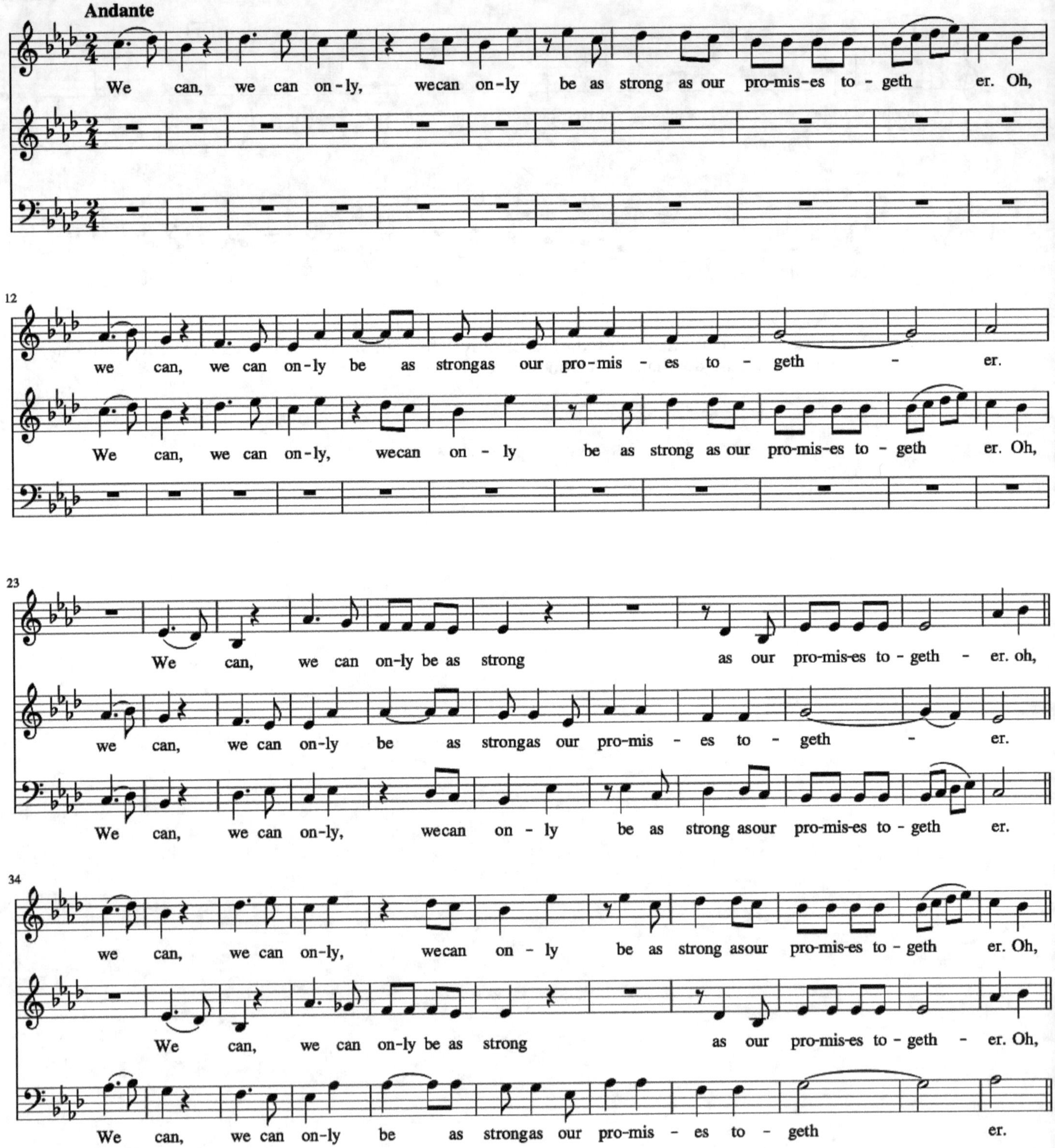

Andante

We can, we can on-ly, we can on-ly be as strong as our pro-mis-es to-geth er. Oh,

12

we can, we can on-ly be as strong as our pro-mis-es to-geth - er.

We can, we can on-ly, we can on-ly be as strong as our pro-mis-es to-geth er. Oh,

23

We can, we can on-ly be as strong as our pro-mis-es to-geth - er. oh,

we can, we can on-ly be as strong as our pro-mis - es to - geth - er.

We can, we can on-ly, we can on - ly be as strong as our pro-mis-es to - geth er.

34

we can, we can on-ly, we can on - ly be as strong as our pro-mis-es to - geth er. Oh,

We can, we can on-ly be as strong as our pro-mis-es to - geth - er. Oh,

We can, we can on-ly be as strong as our pro-mis - es to - geth er.

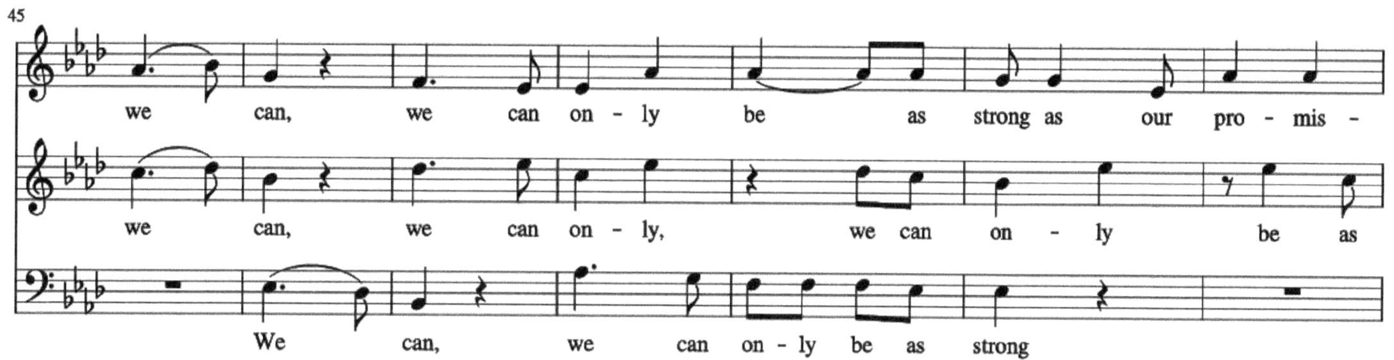
45
we can, we can on - ly be as strong as our pro - mis -
we can, we can on - ly, we can on - ly be as
We can, we can on - ly be as strong

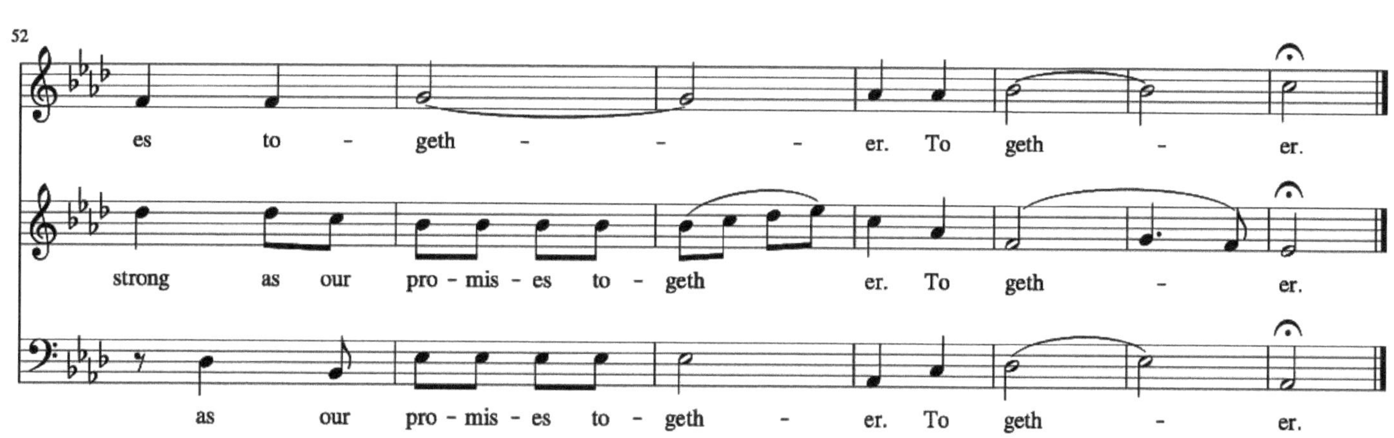
52
es to - geth - - - er. To geth - er.
strong as our pro - mis - es to - geth er. To geth - er.
as our pro - mis - es to - geth - er. To geth - er.

Present Moment

original music
original text

A Three Part Round

Ken Langer

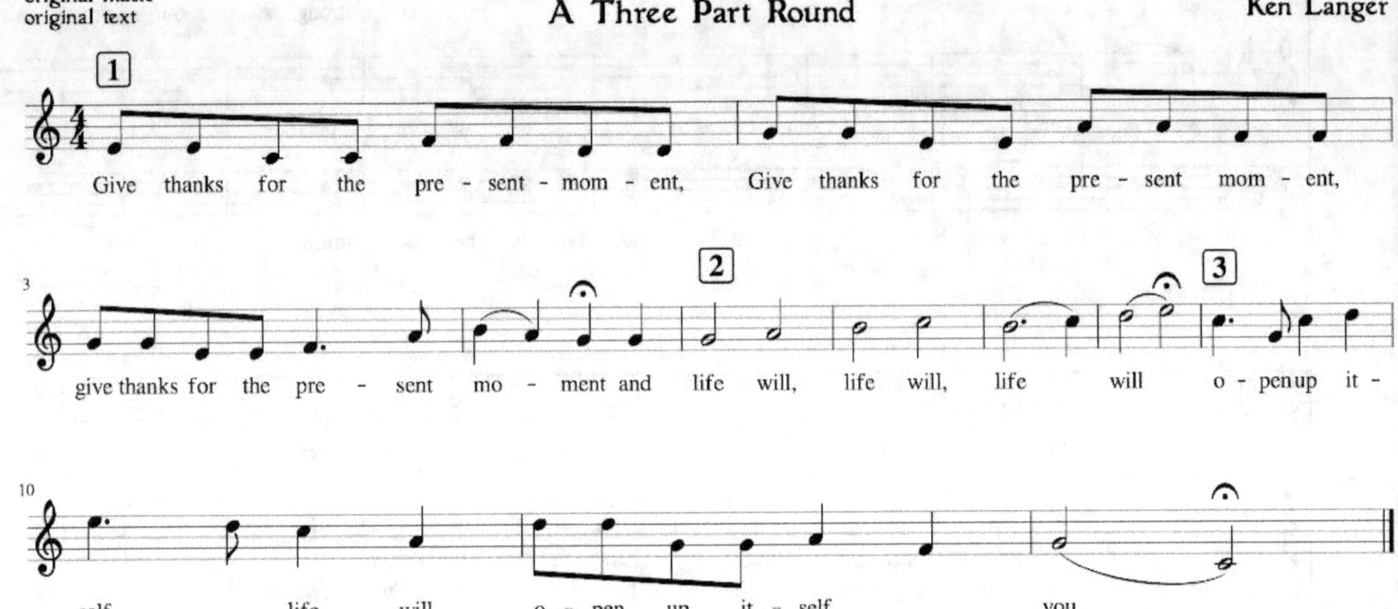

Seek Kindness

music adapted from an anonymous canon
text adapted from Immanuel Kant

A Three Part Canon

Ken Langer

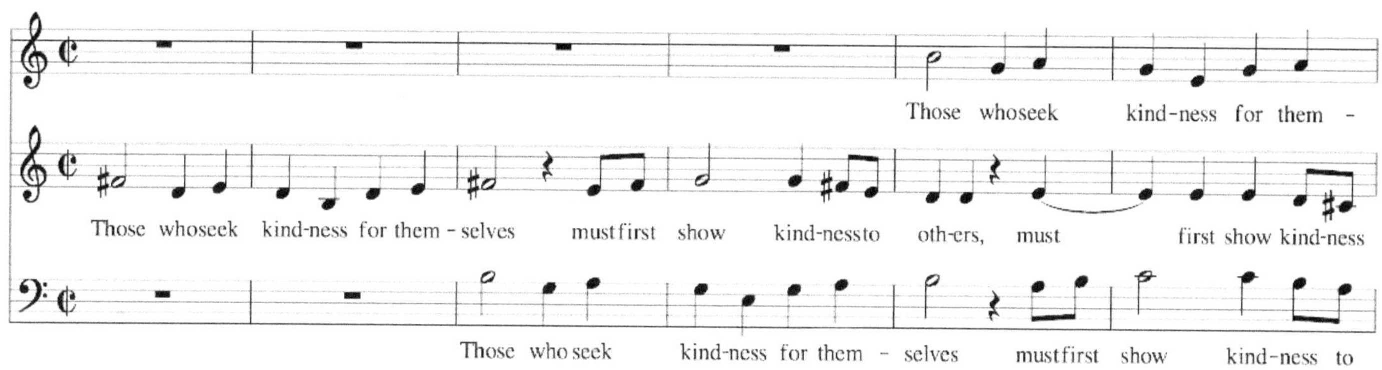

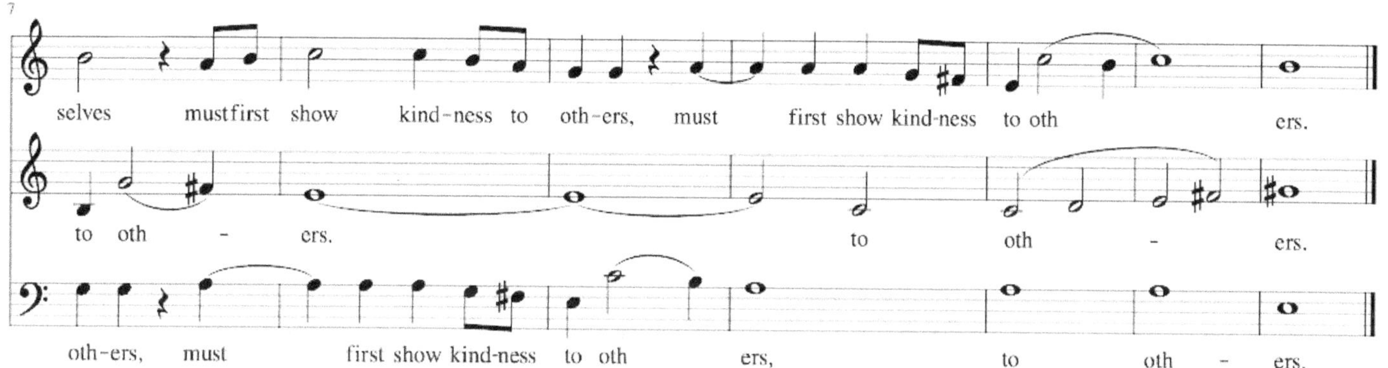

Those people who are cruel to animals harden in their dealings with each other. ~ Immanuel Kant

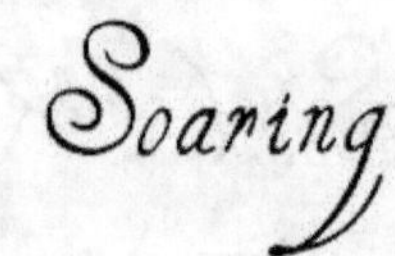

music adapted from Sweelinck
original text

A Three Part Canon

Ken Langer

Adagio

When the young bird learns to fly, when the young bird learns to fly,

When the young bird learns to fly, when the young bird

When the young bird learns to fly, when the young bird learns to fly,

7

fly, learns to fly, it first spreads its wings, it first spreads its

learns to fly, it first spreads its wings, spreads its

fly, learns to fly, it first spreads its wings, it first

12

wings, it first spreads its wings and then lets go, lets go, and

wing and then lets go, lets go. With

spreads its wings, it first spreads its wings and then lets go, lets go,

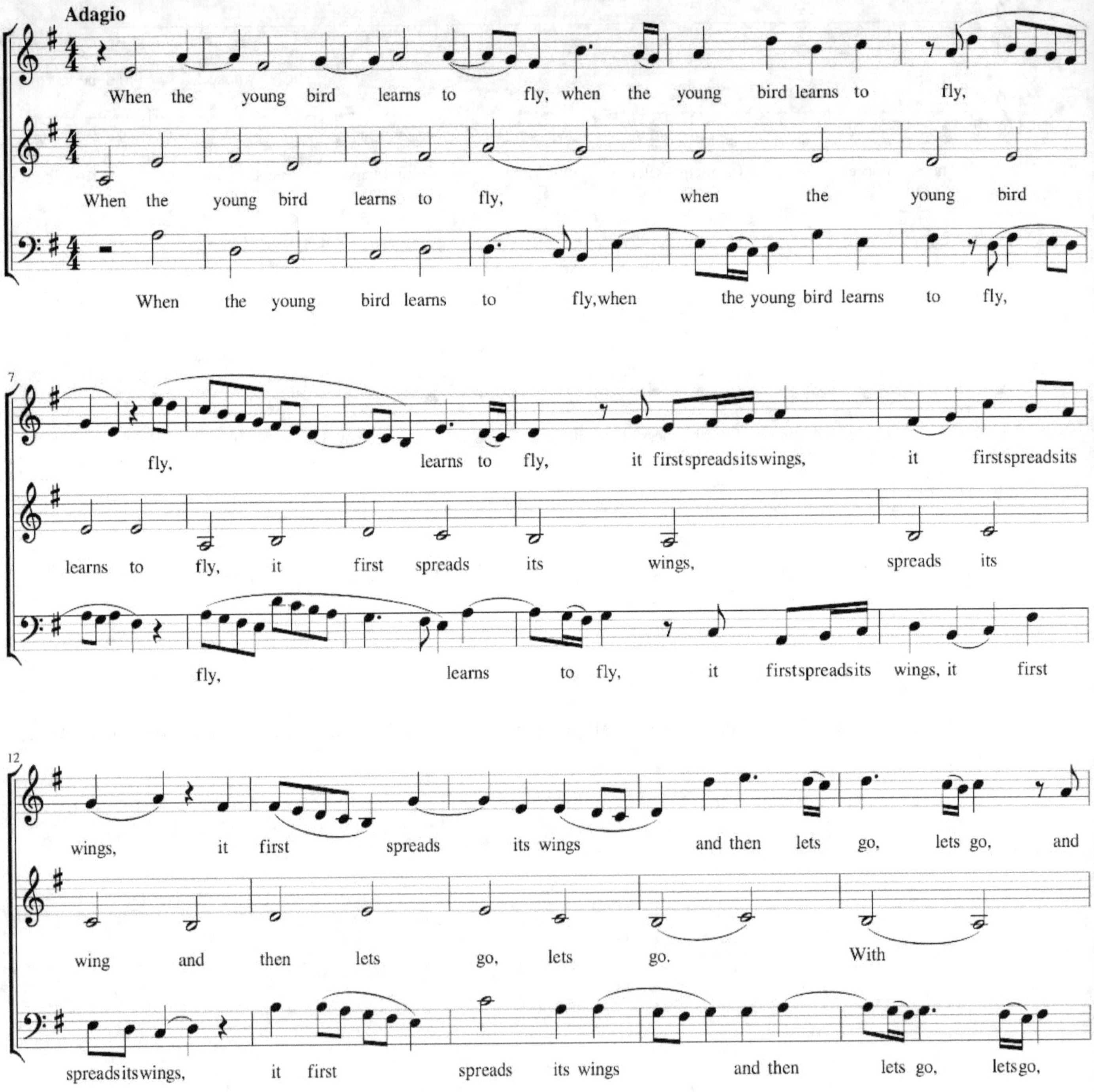

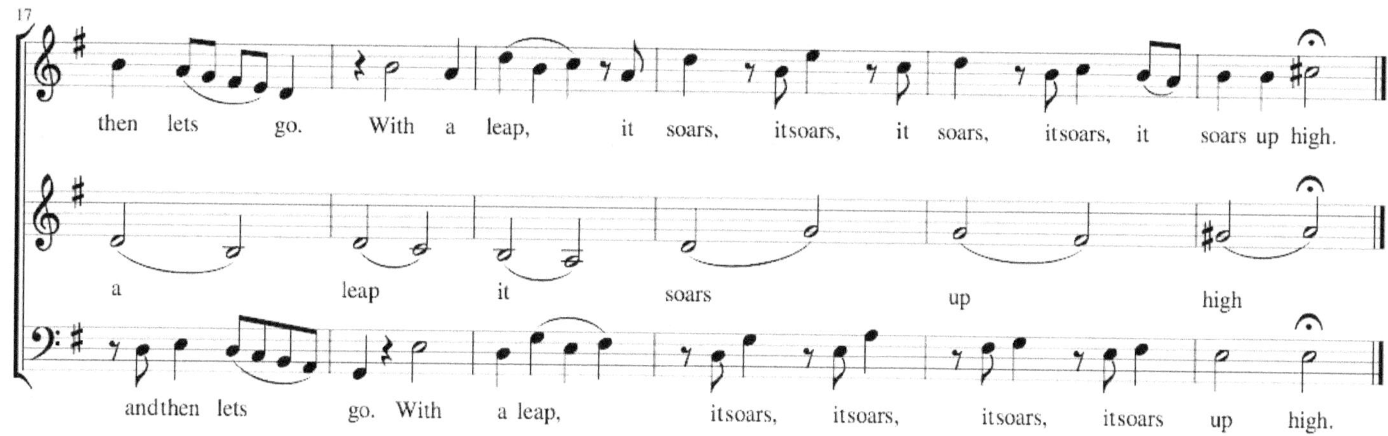
17
then lets go. With a leap, it soars, itsoars, it soars, itsoars, it soars up high.
a leap it soars up high
andthen lets go. With a leap, itsoars, itsoars, itsoars, itsoars up high.

There's a Presence

original music
original text

A Three Part Round

Ken Langer

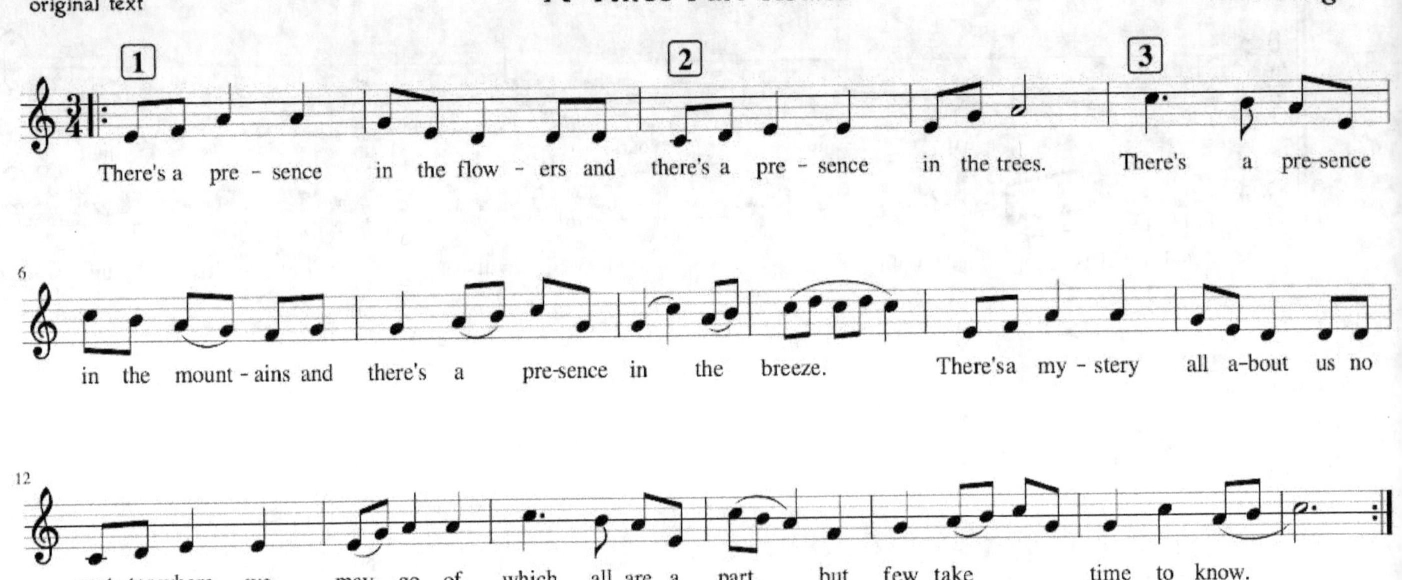

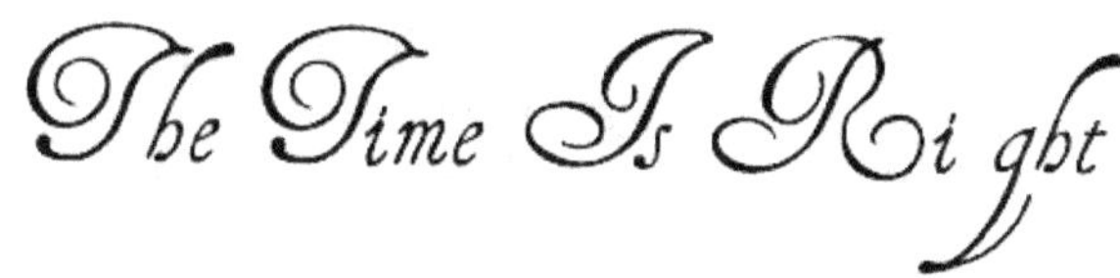

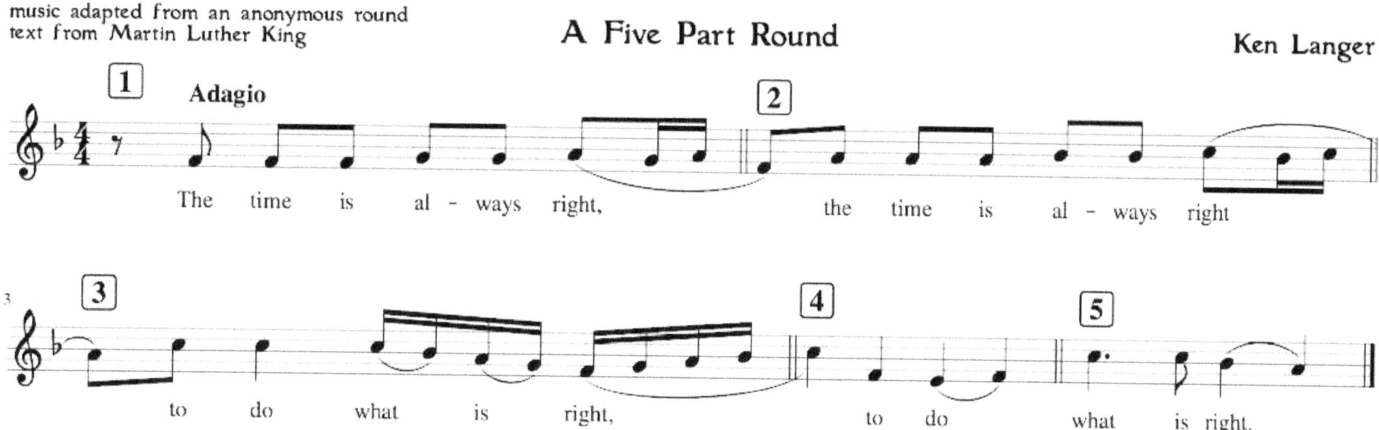

The time is always right to do what is right. Martin Luther King, Jr.

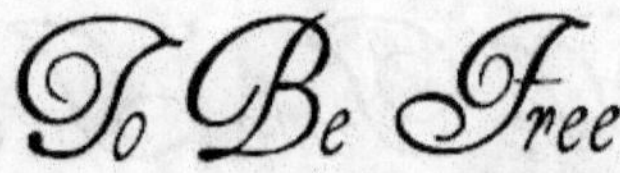

text adapted from Nelson Mandela
original music

A Three Part Round

Ken Langer

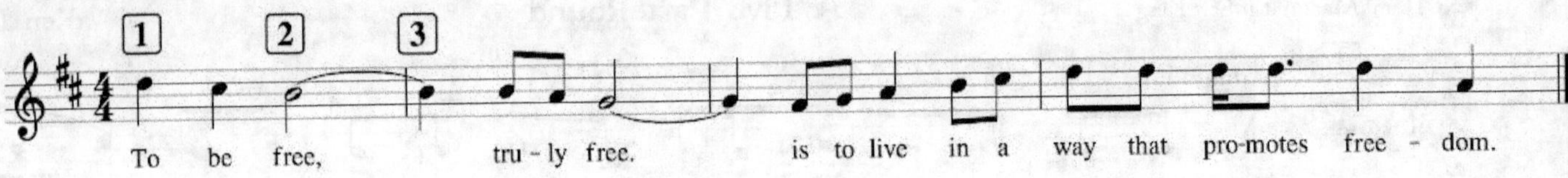

For to be free is not merely to cast off one's chains, but to live in a way that respects and enhances the freedom of others. ~ Nelson Mandela

The True Fountainhead

music adapted from Praetorius
text adapted from Antoine de Saint Exupery

A Three Part Canon

Ken Langer

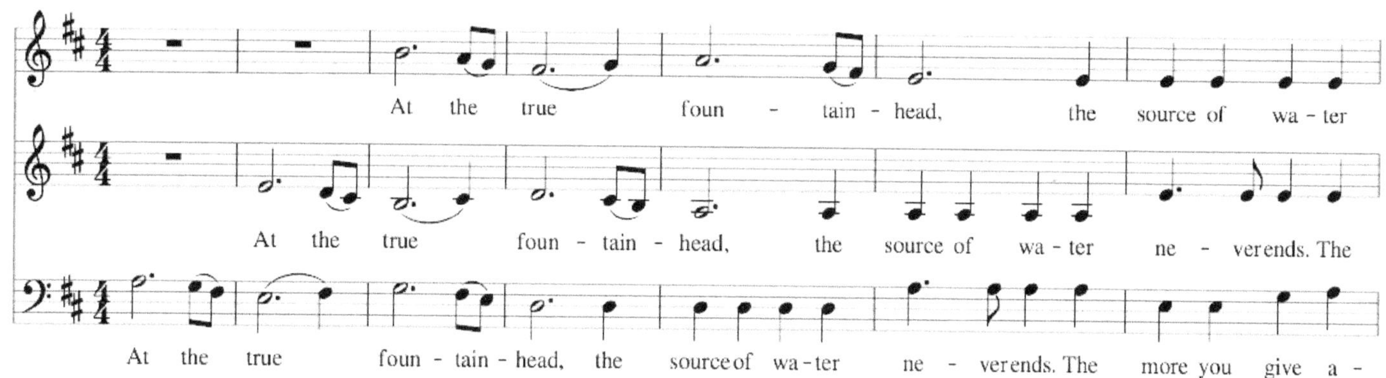

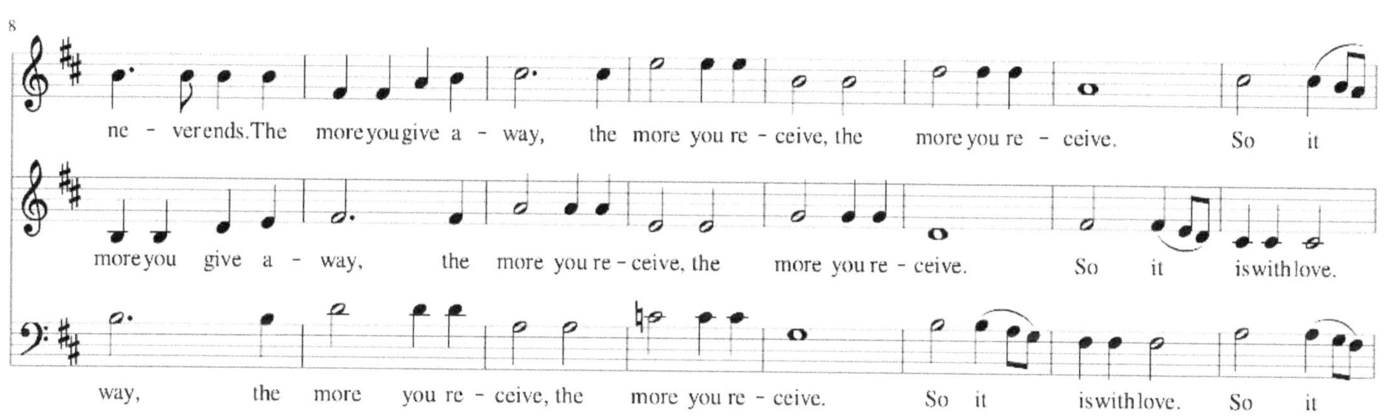

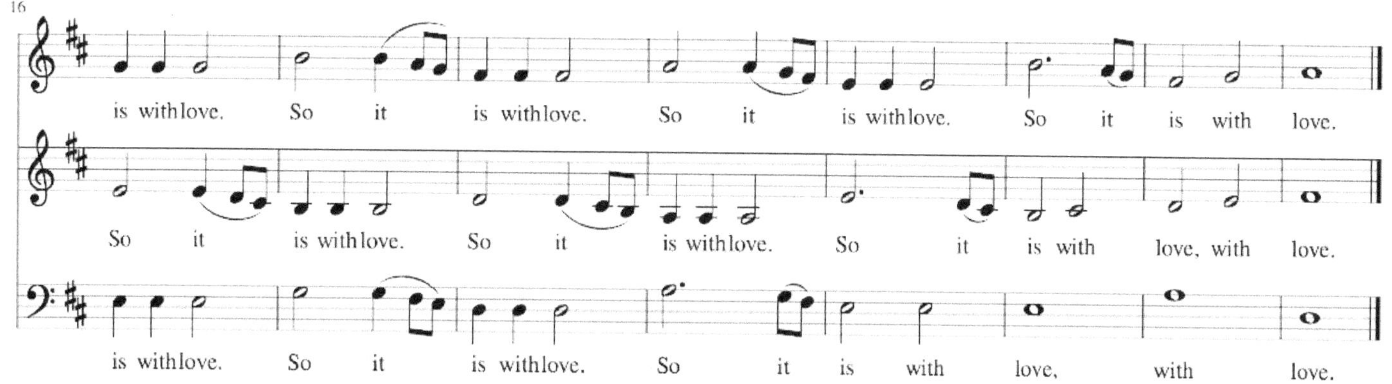

For true love is inexhaustible; the more you give, the more you have.
And if you go to draw at the true fountainhead, the more water you draw,
the more abundant is its flow. ~ Antoine de Saint-Exupery

Ultimate Truth

music adapted from Antonio Caldera
text adapted from Rabindranath Tagore

A Four Part Round

Ken Langer

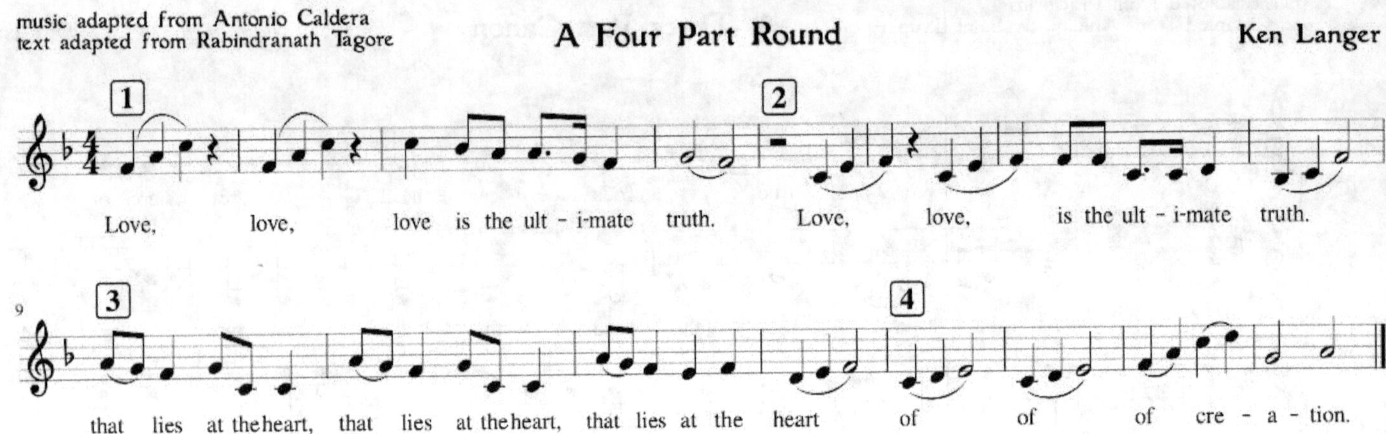

Love is the only reality and it is not a mere sentiment. It is the ultimate truth that lies at the heart of creation.
~ Rabindranath Tagore

The Unfolding

music adapted from Philip Hayes
original text

A Three Part Round

Ken Langer

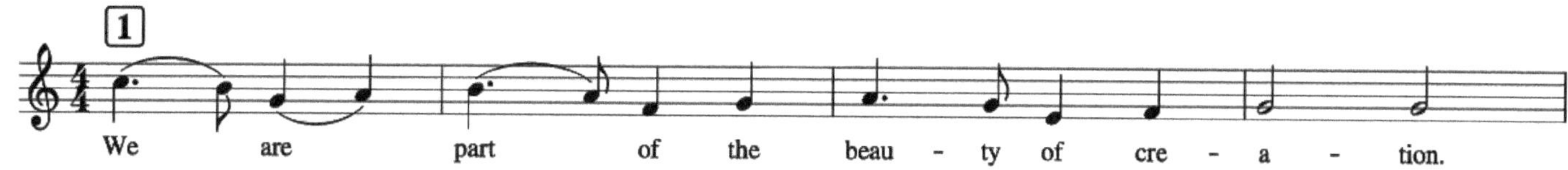

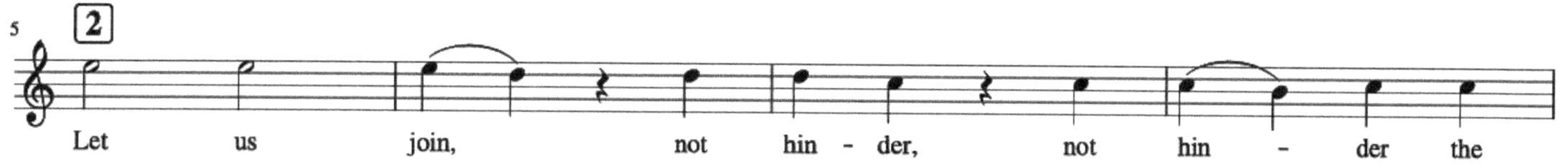

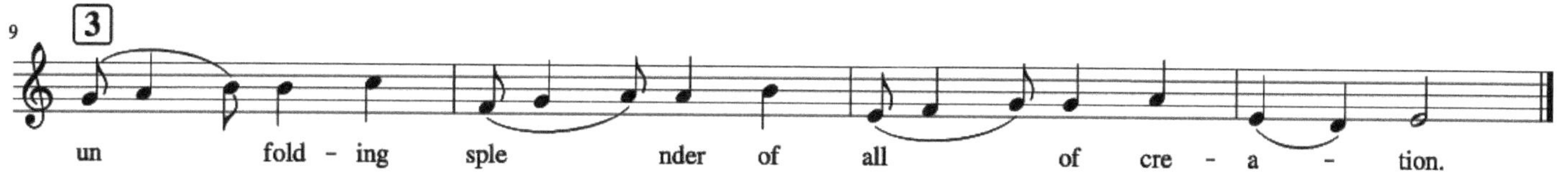

Welcome

original music
original text

A Three Part Jazzy Round

Ken Langer

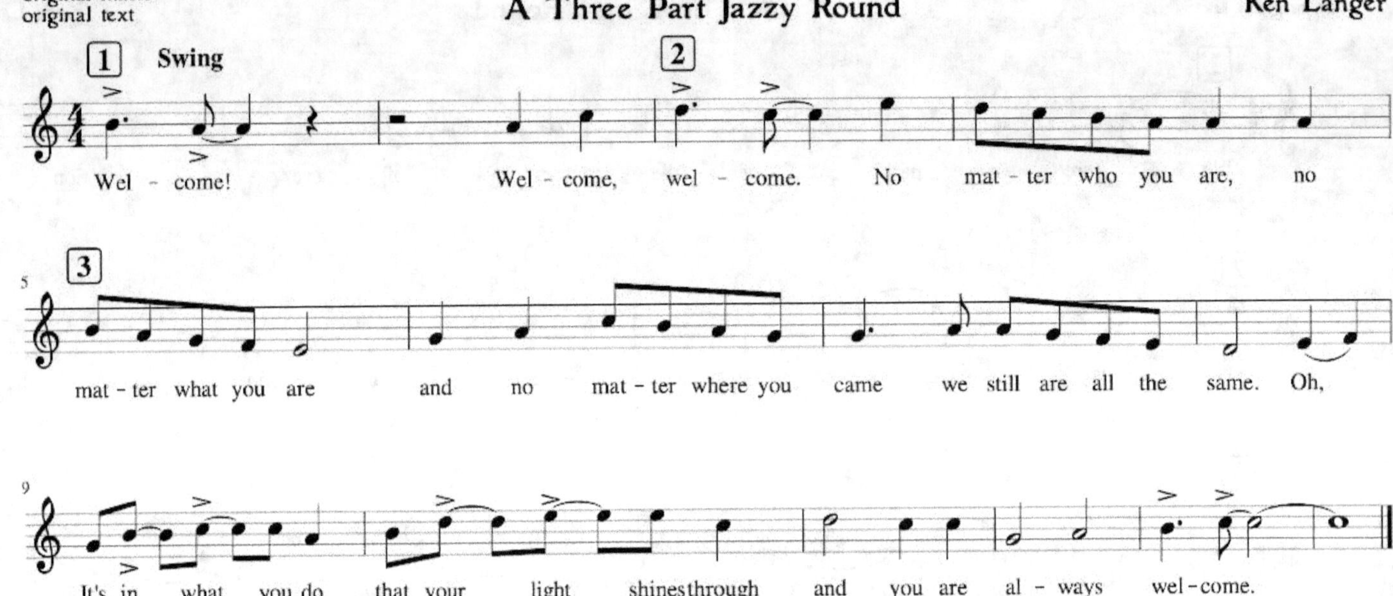

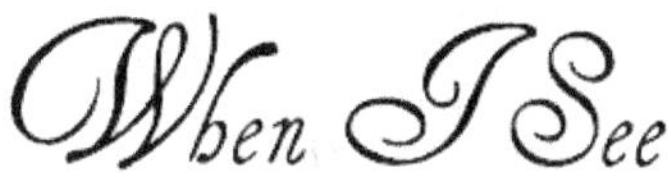

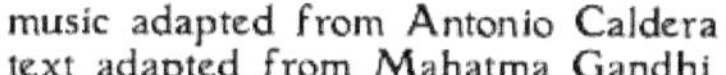

A Five Part Round

Ken Langer

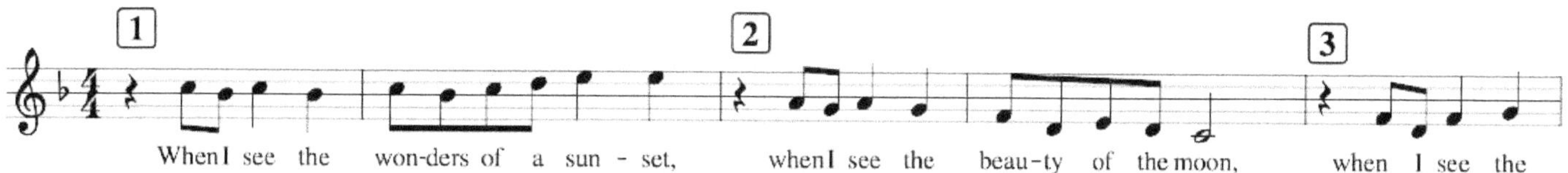

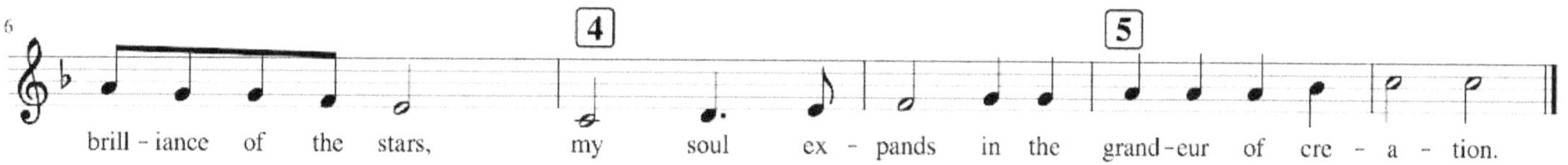

When I admire the wonders of a sunset or the beauty of the moon,
my soul expands in the worship of the creator.
~ Mahatma Gandhi

Appendices

Index of Themes

Index of Forms

Four Part Canon

About the Author

Dr. Kenneth P. Langer lives in the Boston area and is a published writer, composer, and poet and is the author of several works of fiction as well as books on spiritual living. He has commercially published two books and over forty compositions and self publishes many more works. He also enjoys playing and designing games. Learn more by visiting his website: http://kennethplanger.com or contact him at ken.langer@me.com.

Other Music

Several works of music have been assembled into separate books. A listing of those books follows. Many of the scores can be seen and heard at klangermuzik.com or on the Ken Langer Youtube channel.

- Book 1: Music For Piano
- Book 2: Music For Chorus and Piano
- Book 3: Music For Unaccompanied Chorus
- Book 4: Music For Chorus - Various Voicings
- Book 5: Music For Chorus - Smaller Works
- Book 6: Music For Chorus - Holiday Music
- Book 7: Missa Unitas - A Mass For Unity
- Book 8: Dona Nobis Pacem - A Four Movement Work for Chorus and Wind Ensemble
- Book 9: Music For Brass Quintet
- Book 10: Music For Brass - Various Voicings
- Book 11: The Valdemar Experiment - A Chamber Opera based on the writings of Edgar Allen Poe
- Book 12: Music For Strings
- Book 13: Music For Solo Voice
- Book 14: Music For Large Ensembles
- Book 15: Music For UU Choirs
- Book 16: Rounds and Canons for Peace and Justice

Other Books

Non-Fiction

- Spirituality
  - A Different Calling: A Manual for Lay Ministers and Other Non-Professional Facilitators of Any Spiritual Tradition
  - Many Leaves, One Tree: A Collection of Aphorisms Inspired by the Tao Te Ching
  - The Purpose Derived Life: What In The Universe Am I Here For?
  - Three Guidelines for Ethical Living
  - Prayers for a Postmodern World
  - Playing Cards and the Game of Living Well
- Games
  - 52 New Card Games (For Those Old Cards)
  - 36 New Dice Games
  - Forty Games for Forty Dice
- Music
  - A Guide to the Art of Musical Performance
  - A Theory for All Music
    - Book 1: Fundamentals
    - Book 2: Chords and Part-Writing
    - Book 3: The Tools of Analysis
    - Book 4: Parametric Analysis

Fiction

- Science Fiction
  - The Milleran Cluster Series
    - I. Of Eternal Light
    - II. The Forever Horizon
    - III. The Suicide Fire

        - IV. The Song of the Mother
        - The Journey of Awri
- Theater
    - Four Comedies
    - 10 x 10: Ten Ten-Minute Plays, Book One
    - 10 x 10: Ten Ten-Minute Plays, Book Two
- Poetry
    - Looking At The World: A Collection of Poetry

www.ingramcontent.com/pod-product-compliance
Lightning Source LLC
LaVergne TN
LVHW080925110826
845155LV00039B/217
9781949464108